AN ALTERNATIVE GOVERNMENT SYSTEM

INTRODUCING

an alternative government system

- NEW PROVISIONAL INCOME-TAX SYSTEM
- NEW ELECTION SYSTEM
- NEW GOVERNMENT PROCUREMENT SYSTEM
- NEW - REDUCING THE RICH AND POOR GAP SYSTEM
- NEW DIRECTIVE FOR COURTS ON CORRUPTION CASES

AHMED ABU LATIF

authorHOUSE

AuthorHouse™ UK
1663 Liberty Drive
Bloomington, IN 47403 USA
www.authorhouse.co.uk
Phone: UK TFN: 0800 0148641 (Toll Free inside the UK)
UK Local: (02) 0369 56322 (+44 20 3695 6322 from outside the UK)

Published by AuthorHouse   07/09/2024

ISBN: 979-8-8230-8750-6 (sc)
ISBN: 979-8-8230-8751-3 (e)

Library of Congress Control Number: 2024908819

Print information available on the last page.

Any people depicted in stock imagery provided by Getty Images are models, and such images are being used for illustrative purposes only.
Certain stock imagery © Getty Images.

This book is printed on acid-free paper.

CONTENTS

INTRODUCTION

The world has seen significant improvements over the last century, evident in advancements in aeroplanes, cars, trains, ships, buildings as well as in new technologies of mobile phones, computers, electric cars and the list is long.

However, one area that desperately needs reform is the current system of government administration, particularly in developing countries across Africa, Asia and beyond.

The existing government systems are outdated and ill-suited for the demands of the modern era.

These systems lack robust regulatory frameworks, transparency, and accountability.

Consequently, they are riddled with legislative loopholes that foster massive corruption and deliberate mismanagement across various ministries and government agencies.

For instance, a newspaper article from a small developing country reported that thirty percent of the national budget is lost to corruption, equating to millions of dollars.

Here are some disturbing facts about the current government system-

CONSTITUENCY

In many regions, any political party candidate can contest for a parliamentary seat in any constituency.

Often, these constituencies suffer from neglect and underdevelopment because the elected Member of Parliament (MP) is not a local resident and remains disconnected from the area's affairs.

MPs rarely visit their constituencies and are largely absent except during election periods, when they make false promises to secure re-election.

Key Issues –

1. The MP is not from the constituency but from another part of the country
2. The MP seldom visits, leading to constituency's neglect
3. MPs fail to initiate development projects in their constituencies
4. The government does not prioritize the constituency's needs

VOTING AND ELECTIONS

During election years, citizens begin registering a few weeks before the election.

Voting is not compulsory, and the ruling political party often resorts to bribery and false promises to secure votes.

Voters mark their choice on the ballot paper, but due to widespread illiteracy, many votes are nullified.

Additionally, thugs intimidate voters in queues, and the ruling party frequently stuffs ballot boxes.

The election commission cannot verify complaints due to the absence of ID numbers on the ballots.

Voters turnout typically ranges from fifty to sixty percent, with the remaining forty percent either not voting or having their votes invalidated.

Post-election, the losing party often disputes the results, leading to court cases and public protests.

Key Issues -

1. Voters turnout is only 50-60%
2. There is no ID on the ballot paper
3. Bribery of voters is rampant
4. Thuggery in the election queues
5. Vote rigging through ballot stuffing
6. Political parties make false promises

TAXATION

In developing countries, taxation begins when an individual starts a business or service occupation.

They must register for VAT (Value Added Tax) and obtain a tax identification number.

Many transactions are conducted in cash without receipts or invoices (Black Market) to evade taxes.

While established traders and service providers are registered for VAT and other taxes, many do not submit audited accounts to the Income-Tax department on deadline.

Additionally, many wealthy indigenous traders, hawkers, street vendors, minibus operators and private service providers operate without paying taxes, claiming they are below the threshold resulting in only twenty percent paying taxes.

Cross-border trade is poorly regulated, leading to significant customs revenue losses.

Effective legislation needed to ensure tax compliance and increase income tax revenues.

Key Issues –

1. Indigenous wealthy traders should pay taxes appropriately
2. Licensed or unlicensed rural traders are not paying taxes appropriately
3. Hawkers and street vendors are not paying taxes
4. Minibuses, rickshaws, and private taxis are not paying taxes
5. Private sector service providers like barbers, plumbers, mechanics are not paying taxes
6. Farmers with sizeable incomes are not maintaining accounts or paying taxes appropriately
7. Unregulated cross-border importers/exporters (Non Licensed) are not paying customs duty appropriately – selling their goods in Black Marketing
8. Audited accounts are not submitted on time
9. Black Market transactions with cash with no cash sales or invoices to evade taxes
10. Only 14-20% pay taxes

GOVERNMENT PROCUREMENTS FOR MINISTRIES AND PARASTATALS

Large government procurement contracts are frequently awarded based on bribes rather than on merit.

Essential contracts for items such as fertilizers, fuel, medicines, and agriculture products and equipments often go to fictitious companies owned by or affiliated with high – ranking government officials. These companies inflate prices, reduce supply volumes, and cause shortages. Such price manipulations are avoidable.

Additionally construction contracts for schools, clinics, roads and other contracts are awarded to indigenous companies (Non Registered) who often extract funds upfront through bribes, leaving projects unfinished and funds wasted.

Government parastatals , including electricity suppliers, water departments, airlines, operate as monopolies but often run at a loss due to deliberate mismanagement and corruption; instead of generating revenues for government, these parastatals require financial bailouts, which consumers ultimately bear, leading to inflation.

Key Issues –

1. Contracts are not awarded on merits
2. Essential commodity contracts are not given to reputable companies
3. Buildings, roads contracts should not be given to non registered or non reputable companies or individuals
4. Corruption in government parastatals results in significant losses
5. Corruption leads to unnecessary inflation

BANKS

Banks accept large deposits and withdrawal into personal accounts without verification.

BLACK ECONOMY OR TRANSACTIONS WITH CASH

Cash transactions often occur without proper documentation to evade taxes.

Properties, cars, holiday packages, and air tickets can be purchased with cash without raising alarms at the Income-Tax department.

In developing countries almost half of the transaction occurs this way, resulting in substantial revenue loss.

The cross border imports by individuals (Non Licensed) are sold with cash (Black Market) to avoid paying taxes.

Key Issues –

1. Trade transactions are conducted in cash
2. Transactions lack cash-sales or invoice vouchers
3. Properties and cars are brought with cash, evading taxes
4. Cross border imports by individuals are sold in Black market

COURTS

The judicial system is overwhelmed with corruption cases, leading to a significant backlog. Defendants often receive bail and continue in their positions despite facing charges.

Corruption and embezzlement cases though clear, take months or years to prosecute.

Defendants hire top lawyers, bribe witnesses, and influence courts through political connections.

Cases drag on for years without resolution, wasting time and resources and rarely result in the recovery of embezzled funds.

Only about ten percent of embezzlement cases end in conviction

Key Issues –

1. Slow judicial processes
2. Defendants retaining their positions during trials
3. Political interference
4. Witness bribery
5. Immediate bail in high-profile cases
6. High costs of trials
7. Lack of recovery of embezzled funds

HOSPITALS AND HEALTH

Despite significant budget allocations, the main and district hospitals face severe shortages of medicines and beds. The sad fact is that the medicines are robbed by the hospital staff and sold on to black market and some smuggled out of the country. This leads to unnecessary deaths and deplorable conditions.

Key Issues –

1. Medicines are robbed
2. Inadequate bed availability
3. Preventable deaths

AGRICULTURE AND FARMING COMMODITIES

Fertilizers and seeds are priced out of reach for many small farmers due to artificial inflation by dubious companies. These companies import goods cheaply but charge the government exorbitant rates.

The government's laxity, often due to involvement in such schemes, exacerbates the problem.

Effective regulation is critical as agriculture is a national priority.

Key Issues –

1. Artificially inflated prices of fertilizers and seeds
2. Imports handled by dubious companies owned by high government officials
3. Inadequate government intervention

CASH FLOW

Government ministries in many developing countries face cash flow problems, resulting in delayed salaries for civil servants.

To address shortfalls, government borrow locally at high interest rates, further straining finances.

Key Issues –

1. High interest borrowing
2. Delayed salary payments to civil servants

SUING THE GOVERNMENT

Traders/citizens, often with corrupt official's assistance frequently sue the government for substantial claims, such as loss of business or defamation.

These lawsuits, pursued by top lawyers, lead to significant payouts from government, which can ill afford such expense.

Key Issues –

1. Corrupt practices leading to expensive lawsuits against the government.

IMPORTS / EXPORTS

Non licensed individuals import goods at borders and airports, undervaluing them and bribing customs officials to minimal duties.

This results in significant loss. These goods are sold on the black market, avoiding taxes, and the cross border movement of imports and exports remains highly unregulated.

Key Issues –

1. Imports by non-licensed traders
2. Bribery of custom officials
3. Revenues loss from custom duties
4. Black Market sales
5. Highly unregulated cross border trade

SUMMARY:

IN SUMMARY, THE CURRENT GOVERNMENT SYSTEM IS PLAGUED WITH ISSUES, INCLUDING LACK OF LEGISILATION, CONSTITUENCY NEGLET, FLAWED VOTING SYSTEMS, INEFFECTIVE TAXATION, CORRUPT PROCUREMENT PROCESES, JUDICIAL INEFFICIENCIES, FINANCIAL MISMANAGEMENT IN PARASTATALS, COSTLY LAWSUITS, AND UNREGULATED TRADE. THERE IS NO ACCOUNTABILITY AND TRANSPARENCY.

AN ALTERNATIVE GOVERNMENT SYSTEM IS URGENTLY REQUIRED TO ADDRESS THESE PROBLEMS AND ENHANCE THE EFFICIENCY AND INTEGRITY OF GOVERNMENT OPERATIONS.

AN ALTERNATIVE GOVERNMENT SYSTEM

I HAVE DEVELOPED AN INNOVATIVE AND UNIQUE METHOD FOR RUNNING A GOVERNMENT SYSTEM THAT IS PROPERLY REGULATED WITH ACCOUNTABILITY, TRANSPARENCY AND BACKED BY ACCURATE STATISTICS.

I ASPIRE TO JOIN THE RANKS OF GREAT INVENTORS WHO HAVE INTRODUCED TRANSFORMATIVE IDEAS TO THE WORLD, CONFIDENT THAT MY 'SYSTEM' WILL REVOLUTIONIZE A COUNTRY'S ECONOMY WITH INFINITE BENEFITS.

FROM 2005 TO 2012, I DEDICATED EIGHT YEARS TO DEVELOPING THIS SYSTEM.

THE IDEA ORIGINATED DURING A VISIT TO SOUTH AFRICA AT THE HEIGHT OF THE HIV/AIDS PANDEMIC. A BILLBOARD WITH THE MESSAGE "PREVENTION IS BETTER THAN CURE" SPARKED MY IMIGINATION IF I CAN PREVENT TAX AVOIDANCE AND CORRUPTION LEGALLY WHICH LEAD TO THE BIRTH OF A UNIQUE IDEA FOR AN ALTERNATIVE SYSTEM OF GOVERNMENT.

WHILE I AM UNCERTAIN IF ANY COUNTRY WILL ADOPT MY SYSTEM, I HAVE NONETHELESS PROVIDED THE WORLD WITH AN ALTERNATIVE METHOD OF RUNNING A GOVERNMENTS EFFICENTLY, PROMISING INFINITE BENEFITS. THE CHOICE IS THEIRS.

THESE ARE MY NEW CREATIONS FOR RUNNING AN ALTERNATIVE GOVERNMENT SYSTEM WHICH ARE –

1. PERMANENT VOTE ROLL NUMBER OF THE CONSTITUENCY
2. PERMANENT TAX CATEGORY NUMBER
3. TWENTY TAX CATEGORIES
4. UNIQUE FORM C-18 (TO BE FILLED BY ALL CITIZENS FROM EIGHTEEN YEARS OF AGE)
5. UNIQUE FORM 13 (POLICE STATEMENT USED IN CASE OF LOSS BY NATURAL DISASTER)
6. PROVISIONAL INCOME-TAX SYSTEM
7. NEW TAX – TICKET TAX
8. NEW TAX – NUMBERED REVENUE STAMPS FOR SALE OF SECOND HAND ITEMS
9. DUAL TAX – FOR PRODUCE BUY & SELL
10. NEW IDEA FOR REDUCING RICH AND POOR GAP
11. ?
12. ?

THIS IS MY NEW UNIQUE INNOVATION – AN ALTERNATIVE SYSTEM OF GOVERNMENT

CONSTITUENCY:

Every constituent from the age of eighteen years (voting age) will have to compulsorily fill in FORM C-18 at their constituency where they will vote and get a permanent number in the vote roll. The Form C-18 will have to be completed after every five years after the elections. The Form C18 means C for constituency and 18 for eighteen years old. FORM C-18 has four pages.

Page 1: Personal Details

- Constituency where they will vote

- Form C-18 Vote Roll Permanent Number

Page 1: Personal Details

- Constituency where they will vote
- Form C-18 Permanent vote roll number
- Date of registration
- Full Name
- Date and place of birth
- Personal information: education level, health issues, prison records, blood group, HIV status
- Immigration status
- Population Census: household members and age groups

Page 2: Housing Status

- Living in mud/thatched huts or shacks (qualifies for national housing)
- Homeless (qualifies for national housing)
- House type (see chart) Owned or rented
- Trading premises: owned or rented

Page 3 Income- Tax Department**

- Every person will mark on the category of their occupation. There will be twenty categories
- The Income-Tax department will give them a permanent tax number in their category
- A person will have different tax numbers according to their categories
- A person will declare all their Assets, i.e., Properties, stocks, vehicles, jewelry,
- A person will declare all their liabilities, i.e., Bank overdraft, creditors, bad debts,
- Old properties will be revalued to current market prices
- Assets minus liabilities will equal to the person's CAPITAL
- New assessed Income-Tax should be paid for it
- After the above formalities a Tax Clearance Certificate will be issued for that year
- A person can declare their hidden assets in the Amnesty period

This form will ensure comprehensive records for every citizen, aiding in transparency and accountability, and will facilitate tax collections and fraud prevention.

PROVISIONAL INCOME-TAX SYSTEM:

I have *introduced* a Provisional Income-Tax System (PIT) to collect tax upfront across twenty tax categories, each with a different tax rate based on profit margins.

Twenty Percent Provisional Income-Tax

Using a central figure of 20%, the tax rates vary by occupation. For example, a wholesalers 15% profit margin results in a 3% tax rate. This system ensures that tax is collected at the point of sale.

PIT-Collector or PIT-C

Wholesalers issue PIT-C receipts and collect tax from buyers according to their tax rate, recording the transactions on Daily Sales Sheets (DSS). Monthly tax collections are submitted to the Tax Office, which forwards records to the Regional Income-Tax Office (RITO) for accounting.

SPIT Tax Category

All *Service* providers (SPIT) will self tax themselves according to their tax rates. They will NOT collect tax from their clients or customers. The transaction will be recorded on the Daily Sales Sheet (DSS). The DSS will be submitted to the Tax Office monthly with their taxes.

Tax Category Number

All tax categories will have a *Permanent Tax Number* which should be recorded on the Cash-Sale or Invoice voucher. All PIT or SPIT receipts must have the customers Tax Category Number otherwise it will be invalid. One PIT or SPIT receipts number for one Sales voucher number.

The constituency will connect every constituent to the Election Commission to get a vote card number with their permanent number and to the Income Tax department to get a Tax Number in their occupational category.

All trade and service transactions will be conducted using the tax category *number.*

Ticket Tax Ticket (New)

All entry by tickets will be tax prepaid.

Numbered Revenue Stamps (New)

All sales of second hand items will require Numbered Revenue Stamps on the sales voucher

Dual Taxes (New)

Farming commodities will require Dual Tax if the produce or commodity is purchased from the Self Sufficient Farmer (exempt). Dual Tax in one receipt by the buyer and seller.

VOTING AND ELECTION:

The voting process will be streamlined and secure. Registered voters, indentified by their Vote Numbers, will attend designated polling stations. Security personal will maintain order and prevent influence.

At the polling station, voters will present their Vote Cards to the Election Commission officials, who will provide a 4" x 4" card and mark it with the Vote Roll Number, attendance time, and a thumb print of the voter. This will be logged on the Vote Roll.

Voters will then proceed to the polling booth to cast their votes by placing their vote cards into the designated ballot box for their chosen political party, each marked with distinct colors and portraits

Post –voting, ballot boxes will be securely transported to district halls for counting in the presence of party candidates, Election Commission officials, the District Commissioner, Police Chief, and an army representative.

Each box will be opened, votes counted, and results verified by all present before proceeding to the next (party) box.

The final vote count will be forwarded to the Election Commission Headquarters.

BANKS:

The banks will have a company or individuals Tax Clearance Certificate for the previous year; in this way the bank will know that the person or the company are depositing or withdrawing within their means.

The bank will report all suspicious activity to the responsible authorities.

BLACK ECONOMY – TRADE TRANSACTIONS WITHOUT SALES VOUCHERS

In my system, the Black Economy (transactions without cash-sales or invoices) will be eliminated. If it occurs then it will be easily detected with cross checks.

ADDITIONAL TAX REGULATIONS:

Annual Depreciation and Appreciation

Annual Depreciation on all machinery, vehicles, fitting & fixtures etc., will be 10%.
Annual appreciation on buildings, properties (brick & mortar) will be between 5 to 10%.

Late submission of annual audited accounts

If the annual audited accounts are not submitted on deadline then the Income-Tax department will assess the late tax returns directly on the *gross profits*.

Charities

The Income-Tax will not give any concessions on charities. Charities are not regarded as a business expense. This is also to eliminate fraud and tax avoidance, accountability and transparency.

Rental Association

The government will initiate the Rental Association. The Rental Association will be associated with the Income-Tax department. This body will register *all landlords* and give them a permanent number.

All landlords will have to pay twenty percent of their rents received to the *National Housing.*

The workout of rent on the rent receipt will be like this – Rent minus twenty percent for National Housing equals net rent for the landlords. The landlord will pay usual tax on net rent received.

Form 13

This is a new Form that I have created. Form 13 is a *Police Statement* which will record *all losses* by natural disasters for the Income-Tax purporses.

Form 13 will be used to scrutinize **bankruptcy** assessments.

Capital Gains Tax

In my system all *old properties* will have to be revalued at current market value.

Amnesty

Government will allow maximum of two years Amnesty period for all citizens to declare their hidden wealth and pay taxes on them.

No Duty Free Allowance

There will be NO duty free allowance to Charity, Religious bodies, government officials etc.,

CENTRALIZED GOVERNMENT PROCUREMENTS:

Procurements for government ministries and parastatals are centralized to ensure efficiency and oversight, with funds allocated based on essential needs. Tenders are awarded based on merit, and payments are made in stages *after through inspections.*

Contractors and Service providers will adhere to strict regulatory measures.

FAST-TRACK COURTS FOR CORRUPTION CASES:

Embezzlement and corruption cases are expedited, with suspects required to verify assets.

The suspect(s) will stay in remand for fourteen days till they are cleared or convicted by court and income-tax department after through investigations.

Investigation and trials are completed within three to four months.

GOVERNMENT IMMUNITY FROM LAWSUITS:

To prevent dubious claims and corruption, the government *itself* cannot be sued. Instead, individual officials responsible for wrongdoing can be sued.

HOSPITALS:

To ensure hospitals operate efficiently and provide the highest standard of service, a structured system must be adopted. Adequate bed capacity should be ensured at all main and district hospitals.

The Ministry of Health should issue licenses to private pharmacies to establish outlets within these hospitals. Exempt patients would receive three- day supply of prescribed medications from these pharmacies, excluding over-the-counter items such as aspirins and cough syrups.

Inpatients will receive free care, but non-exempt taxpayers will bear the cost of their medications.

This setup aims to streamline operations, with the Ministry of Health funding the pharmacies, thus avoiding the pitfalls of direct medication imports which often lead to mismanagement and shortages.

AGRICULTURE COMMODITIES:

The government must prioritize the pricing and distribution of essential agriculture commodities such as fertilizers and seeds.

Licensed importers should be restricted to a maximum profit margin of twenty percent.

Detailed surveys and data collection within each constituency are necessary to assess the requirements of farmers, regardless of scale. MPs must ensure equitable distribution of these resources.

Additionally, strict price controls on staple foods like maize, rice, cooking oil, flour, and bread are crucial to stabilize the market and protect consumers.

IMPORTS:

Under this system, importers will receive licenses specific to their product categories. For example, a wholesaler dealing in groceries imports will *not* be permitted to import bicycles etc.,

This categorization allows the Ministry of Trade to maintain accurate data on the number of importers and the foreign currency requirements for each category.

Import restrictions or bans on locally produced items will protect local industries and conserve foreign currency reserves.

Proper regulation or cessation of non-licensed imports at borders will also be enforced.

REDUCING THE RICH AND POOR GAP – EMPLOYEES:

The disparity between the rich and the poor must be addressed. Factory workers and laborers often earn insufficient wages despite their hard work, while factory owners and corporate entities grow wealthier.

To rectify this, a policy should be mandate that factories, government parastatals, banks, insurance companies, and farms distribute twenty percent of their post-tax profits among their employees.

This approach ensures a fairer distribution of wealth generated by the labour force.

REDUCING THE RICH AND POOR GAP – NATIONAL HOUSING:

The stark contrast between living conditions of the wealthy and the impoverished, especially in urban and rural areas, must be reduced.

Homeowners, business premises owners, and landlords will contribute twenty percent of their property's rental value (for property owners) or receipts (for landlords) to *National Housing fund monthly.*

These contributions will finance the construction of low-cost housing in constituencies and high-rise flats at city edges, providing decent living conditions for employees and reducing the housing gap.

CASH FLOW:

My proposed system is designed to enhance national cash flow, ensuring sufficient funds to manage the country's needs without resorting to local borrowing.

This will result in significant savings on interest payments, providing financial stability and fostering economic growth.

CONCLUSION:

After comparing the present government system with my 'An Alternative Government System' any un-biased person will agree that my 'system' is much better and effective then the present 'system' in terms of infinitive financial gains, tight regulatory measures, accountability, transparency and a national budget surplus. In addition my 'system' will tax all those who earn, prevent corruption and speed up court cases.

I am proud to present to the world my new innovative 'An Alternative Government System' though a bit late but nevertheless it is here and available.

It will take a courageous and patriotic leader to adopt my 'An Alternative Government System' for their country's infinite benefits.

CONSTITUENCY

THE STARTING POINT OF THIS NEW SYSTEM WILL BE THE CONSTITUENCY

Districts are divided into constituencies, with an elected MP. This is so that the MP can put forward the requirements and projects of his/her constituency in parliament and so develop the constituency.

There could be three to eight constituencies in each district depending on size. These will be known by their positions. For example, Blanmonte district constituency North, South, East or West. But in this system they will be given three initials and a number. Thus, BLT (for Blanmonte) followed by numbers to identify the constituency, such as BLT 1, BLT 2 and so on.

The second most important thing that will be required for the constituency will be a resident MP. The Member of Parliament for each constituency must have continuously lived in the constituency for ten years.

The presence of the MP will be required at all times at their constituency, except when they at the parliament.

Form C-18 is the key to this new system. On it, every citizen over 18-years old will have to fill in their constituency, their personal details, housing, source of income and their capital details.

FORM C-18 WILL HAVE TO BE COMPULSORILY FILLED BY ALL CITIZENS FROM THE AGE OF 18 YEARS.

FORM C-18 may be regarded as a person's history form, since all personal and financial questions will be asked and have to be answered honestly.

Form C-18 Pages 1 and 2 will be for the following purposes:

- They will be used to determine how many voters (18-years plus) are in the constituency.
- They will count the number of people living in the constituency for the purposes of population census.
- It will count the immigrants living in the constituency.
- It will determine what type of house they live in. Are they rented, owned, or is it a mud/thatched hut?

A TEMPORARY C-18 VOTE CARD WITH VOTE ROLL NUMBER WILL BE PROVIDED WHEN REGISTERING FORM C-18.

Form C-18 will have to be filled and registered at the constituency office for all citizens from the age of eighteen. The Form-C-18 will connect all citizens with the constituency where they will vote.

The constituency office will register each citizen and give them a permanent vote roll number and temporary card that will contain the citizen's name, occupation and tax category. Behind the card will be a date stamp and the MP's signature.

The vote card will arrive after all the tax formalities are completed.

At the moment, district constituencies that are especially far from the centre or in deep rural areas are usually neglected, because elected MPs are not familiar with the constituency that they represent. The elected MP is often a complete stranger to the constituency, having contested and been elected on a vacant or available seat. For this reason, many constituencies are never visited by their MPs and not developed. They remain as they are, neglected.

THIS WILL BE THE ROLE OF THE CONSTITUENCY

- There must be a resident MP (a local, who has lived for at least 10 years in the constituency).
- Form C-18 will be registered in the vote roll and the constituent will be given a permanent number. All Form C-18s will go to the Regional Income Tax Constituency Office for tax verification according to the person's occupation.
- The Income Tax Department will notify the constituency office of the persons who are exempt from paying taxes.
- Self-sufficient farmers who own less than $10,000 capital will be classified as a Non-Licenced Holder (or NLH).
- Those in the Exempt Tax Categories will be entitled to free health care and education for their families.
- Self-sufficient farmers will be able to buy subsidised fertilisers and seeds from the constituency warehouse.
- MPs will check the progress of projects in their constituencies and will sign cheques as a third signatory, signalling that work has been done as per schedule or at the required level.
- MPs will oversee low-cost housing projects on the site of the mud and thatched huts in their constituencies.
- There will be a communal home for beggars and deprived persons and boarding for street children in every constituency, which will be sponsored by NH&SWF – National Housing & Social Welfare Funds.
- The hall at the Constituency Office will be used for court sessions, clinics, civic education and adult education classes, as well as postal services, small scale loans or repayments of loan schemes. Each day of the week will be allocated to a particular event and entertainment will be held on Saturdays and Sundays.
- The constituency will provide $100 for funerals to the exempt category and issue death certificates upon the return of the C-18 Vote and Tax Card.
- On the last Saturday of the month, the MP will have a question time for constituents.
- Every five years there will be voting in the constituency and a new Form C-18 will have to be filled in.
- All civil servants' wages and salaries of those working in the constituency will be through the Constituency Office. In this way it will be easy for the Ministry to keep track and uphold accountability.

To understand the new system better, it will be a good idea to explain the whole procedure in full detail, step by step. We will start with Form C-18.

WHAT IS FORM C-18?

Form C-18 is socalled because it is identified by an initial and a figure: the C stands for the Constituency and 18 stands for 18 years.

This form is to be filled by ALL citizens from the age of 18, the age when a person becomes an adult and is eligible to vote.

Form C-18 will record all personal, housing and financial records of individuals living in each constituency, or the full history of the individual.

Form C-18 will be linked to the Income Tax Department to put all citizens into different tax categories, according to their occupation.

On Page 4 of Form C-18, the Income Tax Department will assess all the assets and liabilities of the individual by revaluing all their properties and assets to current market value, alongside the total assets/capital of the citizen.

Form C-18 will also provide the government with the vital statistics for planning and development, on health, education, HIV/AIDS control and treatment/care, for housing citizens living in mud and thatched huts or shacks and provide a population census.

Form C-18 is designed to let the Electoral Commission know the total number of voters in each constituency, including immigrants.

WHAT IS A C-18 NUMBER?

This number will be given upon registration of Form C-18 at the Constituency Office, picked from the Electoral Roll in sequential order.

This number will be a permanent number for as long as the individual is registered in that constituency.

Individuals can only register in one constituency.

This number will be used for identity purposes where required, especially in tax departments, district tax offices and for purchasing or obtaining any governmental services.

WHAT IS THE CONSTITUENCY'S ROLE?

All districts have constituencies. Some large districts have more constituencies; the smaller districts have fewer constituencies.

Constituencies will be given numbers instead of compass positions. For example, the constituency of Blanmonte North will be known as BLT 1 and the other Blanmonte constituency will be known as BLT 2. Three initials will be used to identify the district; in this case BLT stands for Blanmonte.

It will be easier for the government to control the spending, planning the development strategy and distributing aid when there is a need, if it is done constituency by constituency.

There will always be a resident MP in each constituency to look after their constituents' needs.

The voting will take place in the constituency.

DATE OF REGISTRATION

The date on the Form C-18 will be effective until the next registration after five years.

The date is very important because, when the time comes for building low-cost houses in place of mud and thatched huts and high-rise flats at the city borders, those who are registered first will get priority.

The date and the C-18 number are important, as those who register themselves early will benefit from aid/assistance earlier.

NEXT REGISTRATION OF FORM C-18 AFTER FIVE YEARS

This will be counted from the date of registration to the date five years after a general election.

YOUR FULL NAME

Your full name must be written, starting with your first name and second name (if any), then your father's name and your surname.

Each name will have only one C-18 number.

A person may have ten businesses and can have ten tax licence numbers as per their tax categories, but the name and C-18 number will remain the same on the licence.

YOUR DATE OF BIRTH

Date of birth must be stated by all living in the country.

YOUR PLACE OF BIRTH

This must be stated if born in this country.

This information and proof (birth certificate) may be used by the immigration office to determine the residential status of an alien.

This may be used also for birthright purposes by the authorities.

HOW MANY YEARS HAVE YOU STAYED IN THE CONSTITUENCY?

You must state here the number of years you have stayed in this constituency.

This is also for the immigrants with foreign passports.

ALL THE ABOVE QUESTIONS ARE FOR THE RECORDS OF THE ELECTORAL COMMISSION/ CONSTITUENCY AND FOR STATISTICS AND CENSUS

THE FOLLOWING QUESTIONS ARE FOR STATISTICS

EDUCATION LEVEL

This is for a literacy survey in each constituency, and also to establish the fact that candidates for forthcoming elections are literate enough to understand parliamentary deliberations.

The higher the education level the better it will be for the candidates.

The survey will also be about those who can read, write or speak English.

HEALTH: HAVE YOU BEEN HOSPITALISED?

This is for the health survey to determine if the individual has been hospitalised during the year, so that the district hospital can plan to have adequate wards, doctors and nurses to meet demand.

This has become necessary because of the HIV/AIDS epidemic.

PRISON: IMPRISONMENT

This is for the survey on imprisoned citizens living in the constituency and those who are in jail at present (and cannot be counted during the elections).

IMMIGRATION

This is for survey purposes to establish the total number of immigrants, asylum seekers and refugees in the constituency and the questionnaire on the immigrants (aliens) living in this country legally. Also, to determine whether by birthright if they are eligible to become a citizen.

Q1. *Were you born in this country?*
 If the answer is 'yes', this will be considered as a birthright.
 If the answer is 'no', then other residential status may be considered.

Q2. *Were your parents resident here (in this country) before independence? (This is for countries which were under colonial rule.)*
 If the answer is 'yes', then the individual has the right to citizenship or dual citizenship.
 If the answer is 'no', lesser residential status may be granted.

Q3. *When did you enter this country? Give date.*
 Write your date of entry in this country here.

Q4. *Total number of years of residence in this country?*
 Write the total number of years stayed in this country here.

Q5. *Your residential status?*
 Write your residential status here.

Q6. *File number*
 Write your file number here.

Q7. *Your nationality?*
 Write your nationality here.

Q8. *Passport number?*
 Write your passport number here.

Questions One and Two on immigration are there to determine the birthright status to be considered and granted. Also, an individual who has lesser residential status whilst his or her parents were resident in this country, before it became independent, will be considered for citizenship or high residential status – the PRP.

Questions Three and Six on immigration are designed to determine if the immigrant has legally entered the country.

Questions Seven and Eight are there to determine how many immigrants are resident in this country, and where they come from.

After recording immigration, it is time to record the local population as per the constituency in order of their age group and their earning status.

POPULATION CENSUS

Are you the head of the house? Yes/No

The head of the house is the person who is fully responsible to care, protect and look after household needs. The head of the house can be a male or female.

Note: If the head of the house dies and has no will, the assets will be shared by the household members.

Q1. Under 5 years

Write here the number of children up to the age of 5 in the house.

This will provide statistics for the health authorities for immunisations and child care programmes in the constituency also for the education department for nursery, or pre-primary school planning or school places.

Q2. Under 18 and not earning

Write here the number of people under 18 years and not earning a living in this house. The boys/girls may be going to primary/secondary school or college and therefore not earning (or for any reason, as they are free to do as they please and are not answerable.)

In developingcountries it is not compulsory for children to go to school/college up to a certain age/level.

Q3. Under 18 earning/assets

Write here the members of the family who are earning or have assets and are under 18 years of age.

This is also for those under-aged persons who have inherited, and whose estate is managed by trustees/executors.

The Tax department will not be able to tax the under-aged person who is earning but will use the guardian/household head's C-18 number for any taxation purposes.

The trustees'/executors' C-18 number will be used for the under-aged inheritor(s) for any tax purposes.

Q4. Over 18 and not earning

The person will have filled in a C-18 form and stated that he/she are not earning/ un-employed.

The Income Tax Department will classify the person into the Temporary Exempt tax category, giving reasons as:

1. Dependant staying with the family and not earning;
2. Dependant staying with the family and studying;
3. Staying with the family and long-time sick/disabled;
4. Dependent, old age/retired with no assets or earnings;
5. Self-sufficient farmer

There are five types of Temporary Exempt status, as stated above.

These are all temporary exemptions (except numbers Three and Four) where the person will have to seek employment or do something to earn money and register with the Tax Department eventually.

The constituencies' unemployed will be counted in statistics.

If there is any project going on in the unemployed person's constituency, the Ministry of Labour will put them on the employment list as a priority.

They and their families are entitled to free health care and education.

Q5. Over 18 years, earning and holding assets

This person will mark on one of the 20 tax categories as their source of earnings on Page Three of Form C-18.

The Income Tax Department will send them confirmation and a Tax Category Sequence Number. If there is need to register the tax payer with the Treasury Cashier, they will be registered and the Treasury Cashier's location and number will also be given.

This will be fully explained in the Tax Categories section in detail.

The Tax Department will have booklets on each tax category, explaining the workout in full detail.

If the citizen has indicated s/he holds assets in the Assets and Liabilities Section on Page Four of Form C-18, the Tax Department will send them valuation forms as requested.

The valuation forms are the property/assets forms that will be sent out to those who have indicated them. The properties' revaluation will be taxed according to their new market value (see Regulation 22).

Q6. Total number of people in the house

All age groups from Questions 1 to 3 must be added together to calculate the total number of persons staying in each house. Persons in Groups 4 and 5 must be omitted because they will be filling their own Form C-18 and counted individually.

If the family is living in mud or thatched huts, they will be given a low-cost house, with rooms according to the size of the family (in due course).

All questions are for the population census and statistics.

CONSTITUENCY OFFICE WORK

After registering constituents and giving them their numbers from the Electoral Roll, the Constituency Office will give them a temporary C-18 Vote Card.

When the Constituency Office receives Form C-18 from the constituent, it will record all details and pass them on the following authorities:

Regional Income Tax – Constituency Office
Electoral Commission
Statistics Office
Immigration Office
Population Census Office
National Housing and Water Funds Office/Ministry of Housing
Landlords' Rent Association/Income – Tax

For exempt tax categories, the Regional Income Tax Headquarters will compile the names, including the names of the family members and the head of the house C-18 number living with them into a referral type book that will be available to ALL government ministries and constituency offices.

This information will be stored on computer.

CC: Electoral Commission
      C-18 NUMBER – Taken from the vote roll sequence
      CONSTITUENCY – This constituency
      DATE OF REGISTRATION – The day registered
      NEXT REGISTRATION – After 5 years
      FULL NAME – Full name of the citizen registering
      YOUR DATE OF BIRTH – For all persons living in the country
      YOUR PLACE OF BIRTH – For persons born in this country
  STAY IN EACH CONSTITUENCY – Number of years person has stayed in each constituency

CC: Statistics Office
      EDUCATION – For literacy statistics
      HEALTH – For health records
      PRISON – For records purposes
      BLOOD GROUP – For emergency purposes
  HIV/AIDS – To provide medicine/care

CC: Immigration Office
  IMMIGRANT – For statistics purposes

CC: Population Census
  POPULACE IN CONSTITUENCY – Information from the head of the house. Tick 'yes' then count the number of persons living in one house, and add to find total population figure.

CC: National Housing and Water Funds
  Staying in own house / Trading from own premises

CC: Ministry of Housing
      NH&WF – Under this ministry
  Type of house – as indicated

CC: Landlords' Association (rental income)
      Properties – All rented properties in the constituency

FOR THE CONSTITUENCY OFFICE RECORDS

Tax Category – As indicated
Tax Number (if different) – If different then use C-18 NumberOccupation – For statisticsExempt – For free health care, education, subsidised agriculture products, etc.

C-18 PAGES 3 AND 4 WILL BE SENT TO THE INCOME-TAX REGIONAL HEADQUARTERS

All Form C-18s will be assessed and put into tax categories.

The Income Tax Department will inform the Ministry of Home Affairs to issue a C-18 Vote Card or C-18 Vote/Tax Card by issuing a Tax Clearance Certificate for each number.

If the person is classified in the Exempt category, the constituency office will be informed.

MINISTRY OF HOME AFFAIRS

The Ministry of Home Affairs will issue the C-18 Vote Card and C-18 Vote/Tax Card.

THE CONSTITUENCY OFFICE

This office will monitor the Exempt category 1-5.

PROCEDURE AND PROCESS FOR ISSUING C-18 VOTECARD AT THE CONSTITUENCY

1. Upon receiving Form C-18, the constituency will issue a C-18 Vote Card, which will have the following details on the front: (a) full name; (b) C-18 sequence number taken from the Electoral Roll; (c) tax category; (d) occupation.
2. (At the back of the card) there will be a date stamp and the signature of the resident MP.

FORM C-18 IN PROCESS

The constituent will fill in form C-18 and hand it over at the Constituency Office.

The Constituency Office will pick up a number from the Electoral Roll in sequence order and write it in the form.

This number will be with the constituent whilst he lives in the constituency.

The constituent will be issued with the temporary C-18 Vote Card bearing the Electoral Roll number.

If the constituent can be categorised into one of the 20 tax categories by the Income Tax Department, the number for tax will correspond.

If the constituent can be categorised into one of the five exempt categories by the Income Tax Department, s/he will be monitored by the Constituency Office.

The Constituency Office will send the relevant information to the concerned authorities as outlined on Pages 28-30.

C-18 VOTE CARD – REGISTRATION

Upon registering a C-18 at their constituency, each citizen will receive in return a temporary C-18 Vote Card to prove their registration.

The C-18 Vote Card will have the following important information on the front side:

1. *Constituency*
   For example: Blanmonte 2 (actual constituency/number)
2. *C-18 number*
   For example: BLT2/280203 (sequence from Electoral Roll)
3. *Name*
   For example: Ahmad Abu Latif (from C-18 Page 1)
4. *Occupation*
   For example: Bookkeeper (from C-18 Page 3)
5. *Tax category*

For example: SPIT/PROF 1 (from C-18 Page 3)

Rear side:

1. *Date stamp*
2. *Signature of the resident constituency MP*

This C-18 Vote Card will be used until the official C-18 Vote/Tax Card arrives from the Ministry of Home Affairs, when all processing by the Income Tax Department is complete. The temporary card must be returned or surrendered to the Constituency Office.

C-18 VOTE / TAX CARD

The citizen will receive a Vote/Tax Card in due course.

The Vote Card will be used by the exempts during elections for voter identification. The Tax Card will be used by tax payers for transactions for buying/selling and for obtaining services.

The C-18 Vote Card will be required to be shown for all purchases within the 20 tax categories by persons in the Exempt tax category.

The C-18 Vote/Tax Card will be required to be shown for all purchases or services by all the 20 tax categories:

- If the person has been tax categorised, then the Tax Card will be used [1] for election identification; [2] for purchases and services; [3] the Tax Card Number will be used.
- The Tax Card Number in the sequence of their tax category will follow the constituency Electoral Roll number. Example: SPIT-PROF 1/ 786 / 123456BLT2 [bookkeeper].
- If the person has multiple tax cards or has more than one source of income and has, for example, rental income for which s/he is registered, then this is how it will recorded– SPIT-RENT/ 1487 / 123456BLT2
- Any Tax Number will be followed by the constituency Electoral Roll number.

Illustration of C-18 Vote Card – temporary card issued by the Constituency Office:

Front:

1. **Some country government**
2. **Constituency:** Blanmonte 2
3. **C-18 number:** BLT2/123456
4. **Name:** Ahmad Abu Latif
5. **Occupation:** Bookkeeper
6. **Tax category:** SPIT/PROF1/786

Rear:

1. Date stamp of the constituency:	2. Resident MP's signature:

Illustration of C-18 Vote Tax Card:

Front:

1. **Name of the country**
2. **C-18 number:** BLT2/123456
3. ***LSN:** SPIT/PROF 1/786AG
4. **Ministry of:** Accountant General
5. **Name:** Amad Abu Latif
6. **Occupation:** Bookkeeper
7. **Tax category:** SPIT/PROF 1-786
8. **Tax reference No.:** SPIT-PROF1/786 /123456BLT2

The licence sequence number.

The illustration and explanation of the back of the C-18 Vote Tax Card is below.

ILLUSTRATION AND EXPLANATION OF THE BACK OF A C-18 VOTE/TAX CARD.

THIS WILL BE PRINTED AND COMPLETED BY THE MINISTRY OF HOME AFFAIRS AND THE INCOMETAX DEPARTMENT.

STATISTICS

|E   ☐   – Education, if you can speak English write 1, read 2, write 3.

|H   ☐   – Tick here if you have been hospitalised.

|P   ☐   – Tick here if you have been in prison.

|BG   ☐   – Blood group.

|V   ☐   – HIV write 'P' for positive or 'N' for negative.

|IMG   ☐   – Are you an immigrant? Tick here if yes.

|BH   ☐   – Tick here if you were born in this country.

|PHBI   ☐   – Tick here if your parents were here before independence.

HOUSING

	M/T	☐	–Mud Thatched Hut, tick here.
	HL	☐	– Homeless.
	HT	☐	– House Type.
	LIOH	☐	– Living in own house.
	TIOP	☐	– Trading in own premises.
	RI/RS	☐	– Rental Income/Residence.
	RI/CM	☐	– Rental Income/Commercial.

TAX CATEGORY

	PIT- C OR P	☐	– PIT-C or PIT-P.
	SPIT	☐	– SPIT – Category.
	T-TAX	☐	– Ticket Tax Category.
	FRN	☐	– Franchise.
	PAYE- or C	☐	– Pay as you earn orcontract.
	NH&SWF	☐	– National Housing &Social Welfare Fund Contributor.
	NH&SWF Exempt	☐	– NH&SWF exempt tick here.
	EXEMPT 1/2/3/4/5	☐	– Exempt categories 1-5.

ASSETS

| WRITE NUMBERS APPLICABLE | – Write here the assets which the holder possesses. |
| TAX CLEARANCE CERTIFICATE | – This is the total value of CAPITAL VALUE. |

BACK

STATISTICS –	HOUSING –	TAX CAT	– ASSETS TCC
E	M/T		PIT-C OR P
H	HL		SPIT-
P	HTYP		TKT-TAX
BG	LIOH		FRN
V	TIOP		PAYE/C

Form C-18 must be filled and registered every five years after general elections.

1. Form C-18 must be filled and registered every five years.
2. The second registration (after five years) must be after general elections.
3. The five-year interval will determine the wealth of the citizen – its growth or decline.

4. The five-year period will also be an automatic population census.
5. The five-year period will also assess each MP's development projects in the constituency, which must be photographed and recorded.
6. If a citizen wishes to change constituency to the constituency of their choice, they may do so after five years and only after the general elections.
7. The renewed Form C-18 will be compared with the previous Form C-18 to determine (a) growth or decline of wealth and reasons; (b) is the new capital tallying with the tax paid?
8. An enquiry should be set if the figures do not tally or if the tax is not paid adequately.
9. Tax Clearance Certificates with new capital figures will be issued.

ELECTORAL COMMISSION

ELECTION PROCEDURES

The Electoral Commission will have a very important and responsible role in overseeing constituency and general elections.

All constituencies will send in their vote rolls (after recording them) to the EC (Election Commission) to record in their computers.

The Vote/Tax Card will identify tax payers, and those who are tax exempt will have their C-18 Vote Card, which will be used for voting purposes. No other identification documents will be recognised.

During elections, voters will be divided equally according to the number of polling stations to avoid congestion.

Monitors from further districts will oversee the elections under the supervision of the Electoral Commission. At the polling station the voter will hand over their Vote/Tax Card or C-18 Card to the monitor who will highlight the number and write the time on the vote roll as well as on the ballot paper. This is to confirm that the citizen has come to vote. There will be an ink pad at the Registrar's desk and the voter must stamp their thumbprint on the ballot paper before entering the polling booth.

The voter will go in the polling booth and will cast their vote in the party box of their choice, which will have the candidate's photo, party colour and party logo.

The monitors guarding the polling booth (through CCTV) will see to it that only one ballot paper has been cast in the ballot box. The person must not take too long to cast a vote.

All activities in the polling booth will be videotaped for reference.

If a candidate's box is filled up, another box (the same as the previous one) will be replaced immediately.

The boxes will be marked and the ballot papers thoroughly cross-checked with the Vote Roll by the Election Commission when counting the votes.

The votes will be counted from each of the party ballot box in the presence of the Electoral Commission officials, candidates and foreign monitors.

The total number of ballot papers will have to be tallied with the marked Vote Roll.

The winning candidate, as well as the losers, will sign an acceptance of the results.

The counting and total of each box will be passed on to the Election Commission Headquarters.

If everything is to the satisfaction of the Election Commission, then, and only then, will the results be announced.

ELECTION COMMISSION: VOTE ROLL C-18 NUMBERS

VOTERS' LINE OR QUEUE

Voters will queue up at the designated polling station according to the specified numbers on their Vote/Tax Card. For example, Numbers 1 to 600,000 at Polling Station A and 600,001 to 1,200,000 at Polling Station B etc.

VOTERS REGISTERING AT THE POLLING STATION

Voters will show their Vote/Tax Card to the polling station official who will highlight the C-18 Number on the Vote Roll and write the time of the person's presence. The ballot paper will be handed out to the person to go to the polling booth to cast their vote. The ballot paper will bear the C-18 number and time on it.

VOTERS INSIDE THE POLLING BOOTH

The voter will have a look at the candidates' photos and the party they represent with their party colours, name and logo on each ballot box, before deciding whom to vote for. They must not take too much time to vote.

CONSTITUENCY POLITICAL PARTY CANDIDATES

TO QUALIFY FOR PARTY CANDIDACY (REQUIREMENTS):

The candidate must be over 30-years old.

He/she must be educated up to primary level. (Since there may be many uneducated persons in the districts who are wise and mature.) Higher education level will be an advantage.

He/she must not be a known controversial person.

He/she must not have a criminal or police record.

He/she must be approved by the (a) District Magistrate (b) District Commissioner (c) District Police Commissioner (d) Official of the Ministry of Home Affairs (e) Official of the Election Commission.

Five candidates from different parties will be allowed to contest the elections in each constituency.

The candidate must be originally from the constituency they will represent in parliament.

POLITICAL PARTIES' PRESIDENT'S LOGO WITH THE CONSTITUENCY CANDIDATES' PHOTOS ON BALLOT BOXES

There will be a photo of the contesting parties' president and the candidate's photo with party logo on ballot boxes.

There will separate ballot boxes for every party.

The counting of votes will be done at the constituency hall, in presence of the party candidates. All the candidates with the Election Commission officials and foreign monitors will have to sign the results of the vote count.

The candidate representing the party must come from the constituency, having stayed there for ten years.

ELECTION PROCEDURES

The Electoral Commission will be appointed by the Supreme Court to oversee elections and not by the ruling president.

The Electoral Commission will invite foreign monitors for each district in the country.

The EC will engage the army and police or any other citizen to observe and regulate voters at polling stations.

The EC will order the presence of armed soldiers and policemen at each polling station – and also be with the ballot boxes as they are transported to the district's constituency hall for counting.

THE DUTIES OF OFFICIALS AT POLLING STATIONS

There may be one, two, three or more polling stations in each constituency, depending on its size.

Citizens must know their polling station as it will be marked on their C-18 Vote/Tax card. The marked polling station is where they will be able to vote.

Voters will appear at the polling station and be in a queue. When their turn comes, they will show their C-18 Vote/Tax Card to the monitoring EC official at the desk.

The official will inspect the C-18 Vote/Tax Card to see if the voter is at the right place and then will give the voter a ballot paper after marking their C-18 Vote/Tax Card number on the front, and the time of their presence on the ballot paper. The same thing will be marked or highlighted on the Vote Roll. The voter will thumbprint the ballot paper in front of the official.

Voters will then go inside the polling booth with their ballot papers, where they will choose their party candidate for the constituency. There will be ballot boxes of every party with photos of the political party's presidents with their party colour, logos or emblems. The voters will put their ballot paper in the party box of their choice.

Inside the polling booths video recording will be in progress. The video recording will be monitored by the Electoral Commission with the foreign observer next to the polling booth.

COUNTING VOTES

1. Counting of votes will take place at the district's constituency hall, taking votes from each ballot box.
2. Ballot papers will be tallied with the Vote Roll by a different coloured ball point pen or colour pencil by ticking it. All candidates will have different colours.
3. Candidates will have to be present at the counting with the EC officials and foreign observers.
4. Candidates will have to sign and confirm the count.
5. The EC officials will pass the results to the EC Headquarters.

WHATS NEW WITH THIS SYSTEM? IRREGULARITY DETECTION

1. Writing of each Vote/Tax Card number and the time on the ballot paper must be tallied with the Vote Roll when counting votes. If there is any irregularity it will be easily detected. (This is a new system.)
2. Recording the time on ballot papers. In the event of a dispute, video recordings are to be referred to. (This is new.)
3. Voter's thumbprints on the ballot paper. To be checked in the event of dispute. (This is new.)

4. Ballot papers to be kept secret until the day before the election, so that the ruling party may NOT get a chance to print them. (This is new.)
5. The video recording can also count the voters. To stop anyone stuffing forged ballot papers and showing high numbers of turn out from the actual figures. (This is new.)

THE NEW MEASURES FOR ANTI RIGGING ARE:

- Writing the Vote/Tax Card number on the ballot paper and Vote Roll.
- Recording the time of attendance on the ballot paper and Vote Roll.
- Voter's thumbprint on the ballot paper.
- Video recording in the polling booths.
- Separate ballot boxes for each candidate.

THE ROLE OF AN ELECTED MP

1. MPs will have all the statistics of their constituents: the unemployed, the homeless, self-sufficient farmers, the total numbers of mud and thatched huts, the number of taxpayers, employed, businessmen, civil servants, privileged home and commercial property owners who will be the contributors for the National Housing and Water Fund and ongoing projects (if any).
   - The MP must try to bring in some useful projects and develop the constituency and sort out any outstanding issues.
   - The MP's role will be to improve the conditions of their constituents in ALL sectors.
2. The MP will receive copies of bills that are to be tabled in parliament and the MP must deliberate on them when the time comes. The MP can also put in proposals for their constituency needs.
   If an MP has any doubts or is undecided on a forthcoming bill of national importance, they will be allowed to consult five to seven persons from within their constituency for advice or consultation.
3. Elected MPs will be allowed to choose proxies if they are selected to be in the capital city on ministerial duty or on a certain committee post.
   The MP will be responsible for all decisions regarding their constituency.
   The proxy may run the day-to-day affairs.
4. The MP will play a major role to oversee the building of low-cost housing in place of mud huts for their constituents. This will be sponsored by National Housing and Water Fund or NH&WF. The MP will have to make a report of progress.
5. If the government decides to subsidise agriculture commodities, the MP will have relevant data of each constituent's needs and will distribute accordingly.
6. If there is any development project going on in the constituency, the MP will inspect the completed work and will sign it off upon completion.
7. The MP will be the third signatory on bank cheques when they are released to the contractor for payment.

PERKS AND DO'S AND DON'T'S FOR MPS

In every constituency there will be:

- Offices for the MP/secretary/clerks.

- A police post.
- A warehouse.
- A large recreation hall where educational films will be shown. The hall will also be used for other entertainments as well. The hall will also be used for meetings/weekly court sessions /weekly medical visits.
- There will be an official residence for the MP.
- There will be an official seven-seat vehicle for the constituency, which will also be used as an ambulance.
- There will be an official vehicle for the MP.

WHAT THE MP IS ALLOWED TO DO

The MP is allowed to call five to seven persons from their constituency to discuss issues of national importance.

The MP will have a question time at the hall once a month.

WHAT THE MP IS NOT ALLOWED TO DO

- Interfere in police investigations.
- Intervene on behalf of a constituent in court cases.
- (Opposition MPs) WILL NOT be allowed to join the ruling party's government.
- To take the law into their own hands.

PRESIDENTIAL ELECTIONS

There will be no separate ballot paper to choose the president.

The party which has most MPs will form a government.

If there is no clear majority and coalition is required, then the rules of the land will apply.

PENALTIES FOR NOT VOTING

EXEMPT TAX CATEGORY: Will be deprived of privileges offered in that year.

CIVIL SERVANTS: 20% of their salary will be deducted as a fine.

ALL OTHERS: Will be fined from $100 to $2,000 according to their capability.

NATIONAL HOUSING AND SOCIAL WELFARE FUND

LOW-COST HOUSING

The National Housing and Social Welfare Fund will be the organisation that will be created to build low-cost housing of brick, cement and iron sheets on the spot of the mud and thatched huts. The organisation will also dig water boreholes, pay for the funerals of tax exempt citizens and will also give soft loans to tax exempt citizens during lean periods.

The contributors to the low-cost houses will be by privileged families living in their own residence, or trading or providing services from their own premises. They will contribute 20% of the rent, equivalent of the market value, to the National Housing and Social Welfare Fund.

National Housing and Social Welfare Fund will have its headquarters in the capital and will have offices in all the districts.

The landlords will also be the contributors of twenty percent of their rent collected towards the NH&SWF. This contribution is not tax claimable.

The low-cost houses will be built and distributed in sequence order of C-18 registration.

The government will not fund this project, but the law will be enforced for this important legislation.

Proprietors using their own residential/commercial premises will pay 20% of the rent equivalent to the NH&SWF; it is because the property owned and used by them does not generate income tax from rentals, and does not benefit the government. Therefore, the 20% rent equivalent contribution may be used in helping the less fortunate mud and thatched hut dwellers and persons living in shacks in the cities.

The NH&SWF will use and spend money on contracts from the funds available and not borrow.

REPLACING MUD-THATCHED HUTS WITH LOW-COST HOUSING
BUILT WITH BRICKS, CEMENT AND IRON SHEETS

The government's policy will be to demolish all the mud and thatched huts in rural villages and build in their place new low-cost housing, built with bricks, cement, and iron sheets. This low-cost housing will be given free to them.

Low-cost housing and water well projects will be funded by property owners who live in their own residences and conduct business and services from their own properties/premises. Or, by those who live in their own residential/commercial property and don't pay rent.

The amount of the contribution per month will be based on the rent prevailing in each particular type of property in the local area.

20% thereof will be a compulsory contribution towards the NH&SWF.

The theory behind the 20% contribution is based on the fact that if each property had been rented, the Tax Department would have benefitted by receiving 20% tax.

The government will not be responsible for funding these projects.

The projects will be carried out if the funds are available and will not borrow.

The NH&SWF will also build flats at the edge of the cities for the workers, to accommodate them at one fifth of the prevailing rent.

LANDLORDS: Landlords will contribute 20% to the NH&SWF for the rent received. Supposing the rent is $100 per month. The landlord will issue a receipt; there will be two receipts in one [dual]. On the top part of the SPIT-RENT # receipt from which the Landlord will contribute 20% to the NH&SWF. On the second part the Proprietor will pay SPIT on the NET rent.

NATIONAL HOUSING AND SOCIAL WELFARE FUND

Many people in developing countries' rural areas live in mud and thatched huts with low paid workers living in shacks at the borders of the cities as they cannot afford to build houses with bricks, cement and iron sheet roofing.

For these purposes, a formula for building low-cost houses in place of the mud and thatched huts has been established and also to build high-rise flats.

Funding is essential to this project, but the government cannot help as the national budget cannot accommodate it.

These projects can be funded locally by privileged residential and commercial property owners and landlords.

ROLE OF THE NATIONAL HOUSING AND SOCIAL WELFARE FUND

1. To build low-cost houses of bricks, cement and iron sheet on the spot of mud thatched hut and low rent flats for workers in the cities.
2. To dig water boreholes in villages where needed.
3. To pay for the funeral expense of tax-exempt citizens.
4. To give soft loans to the villagers/constituents in lean periods.

This organisation will have its headquarters in the capital and offices in all districts.

Constituencies will send to the district NH&SWF office a list of families that require low-cost houses in sequence order of their C-18 registration.

The Income Tax Department will send a copy of the potential contributors list to the NH&SWF headquarters for pursuance.

All contributions collected will go to the headquarters bank account and the NH&SWF will distribute the funds to each district office accordingly.

Water well projects will also be planned and implemented where required in villages.

This is a very ambitious project, which will do the country proud and balance the wealth contribution from the privileged rich to poor citizens.

The NH&WF will survey the cost of the low-cost houses and categorise them into three groups:

1. LCH- 2: Two room house.
2. LCH- 3: Three room house.
3. LCH- 4: Four room house.

The NH&SWF will know exactly how much each house costs.

The NH&SWF will know the exact cost of all low-cost houses and will allow contractors a 20% profit margin as per regulation 8.

Inflation rates will be considered [every year] and prices will be increased to maintain the level of profit at 20% for the contractors.

WATER WELLS OR BOREHOLES

The government will consider having water wells in villages where there is need.

The water wells will be built with the National Housing and Social Welfare Fund.

The NH&SWF will identify/earmark villages where there is a need and will contract the projects.

The water wells will be budgeted alongside the low-cost housing scheme.

The water wells will be done only if there are funds available.

The water wells will not be contracted on credit terms.

The water wells should be placed in a central position in order to benefit the whole community.

The water wells will be funded by privileged residential and commercial premises owners and landlords.

FUNERALS

The NH&SWF will pay $65 towards the funeral for those in exempt categories 1 to 5 provided that the C-18 Vote Card is returned/surrendered.

Death certificates will be issued at the constituency office and crossed off from the Vote Roll.

SOFT LOANS IN LEAN PERIODS

There comes a time in a year when, prior to cultivation, there is a lean period where there is a dire need of food. In this period the NH&SWF should hand out funds to see citizens through the period. This fund can be free or loaned.

Citizens will be exempt from paying to the NH&SWF if:

1. Residence only mortgaged property.
2. If the 65-year-old male or 60-year-old female are living in their property with their dependants.
3. If the total household earnings are less than $2,000 per month or the house is worth less than $10,000.
4. If the house value is less than $40,000 at the current market value.

QUESTIONS AND ANSWERS: NATIONAL HOUSING AND SOCIAL WELFARE FUND

Who contributes?

Contributors will be homeowners and commercial property owners who work from their premises and do not pay rent for it and landlords.

How much will the contribution be?

20% of the prevailing rent.

For example, if the prevailing rent of the house is $100 per month, then the contribution towards NH&SWF @ 20% will be $20. Therefore, $20 will be the monthly contribution of the house owner to the NH&SWF.

Landlords will contribute 20% of their rental to NH&SWF.

Where will the NH&SWF office be and where will the contributions go?

The contributions will go to the NH&SWF District Office.

What will the NH&SWF do with the contributions?

The NH&SWF will build low-cost houses in rural areas in place of mud huts, dig boreholes for water where necessary and also pay $65 towards funeral costs to tax exempt citizens whose relatives will return their C-18 Vote Card.

How soon will the low-cost houses be built?

It will depend on the funds available. Those who were first registered in sequence order on the Vote Roll will get the low-cost house first and those who registered later will get their low houses later.

Will the low-cost homeowners pay rent?

NO. The low-cost house built on the spot of their mud hut will be free.

Will the flats built by the NH&SWF in the towns or cities pay rent?

YES. They will pay 20% of the rent prevailing. Supposing the landlord elsewhere is charging rent at $100pm then the NH&SWF flats will be rented at $20pm.

Who will be exempt from contributing to the NH&WF?

- Households whose earnings are less than $2,000 per month.
- 65-year-old males and 60-year-old females who live with their dependants.
- Those whose houses are on mortgage.
- Those living in residences whose value is less than $40,000.

Are the contributions by the house/commercial property owner subject to tax claims?

NO. The contributions are **not** tax claimable.

TYPES OF HOUSES AND THEIR CODES.

1/2/3/4/5 = BEDROOMS
FNC = FENCED
GRG = GARAGES
SWM = SWIMMING POOL
GAR = GARDENS

(LCH) HOUSE TYPE: LOW-COST HOUSES BY NH&SWF

Rent per room to be determined by the NH&SWF.

(QUR) QUARTERS

Provided by employers on a no rent basis.

(RBS) RESIDENCE ON GROUND FLOOR BEHIND SHOPS

In smaller towns there are residences behind shops.

(FLT) FLATS

All types of flats with one, two or three bedrooms.Most flats have two storeys.

(BNG) BUNGALOWS

In residential areas of towns/cities.

(MNS) MANSION

A large house with over six bedrooms.

1. For example: A bungalow that has three bedrooms and is fenced with a garage and has a swimming pool and a garden will be written up on the Form C-18 Page 2 house type section as follows:
   BNG 3/FNC/GRG/SWM/GAR.
2. Rent will be determined as and when necessary by the authorities.
   (This is for the NH&SWF 20% contributions.)
3. If an employee stays in a company house, his residence will be called 'Quarters'.
   This will be valid if the employee pays no rent.
   The employee will write in the Quarters box the type of house they are living in.

LIVING IN OWN RESIDENCE

This is for families living in their own residence and paying no rent in the rural districts or urban areas.

The whole process is useful for statistics and NH&SWF records.

The following information will have to be written on the Form C-18 Page 2 in the 'Living in Own Residence' section.

(Plot number)

Plot number should be written here.

(Deed number)

Deed number should be written here.

(Street/Location)

Write here the name of the street or any name the place is known by.

(Location in the constituency)

The location usually has a name. Write the name here, or the local place name.

(City rates reference number)

This is most important as the city will charge the owner rates on the plot/developments. This will help the relevant authorities to cross check. The city rates reference number should be written in this space.

(Water meter reference number)

Write in the space the water meter or account number.

(Prevailing rent per month of the area/location)

This is to be assessed by the NH&SWF and the owner/proprietor will be informed/notified in due course. (This is when areas have been surveyed and the tax authorities contacted to determine the average rental income prevailing at the point of time in the particular area/location.)

Contributions by the proprietors are NOT tax claimable as a business expense. Twenty percent rent contribution to the NH&SWF can be worked up in the capital account like drawings account.

THERE WILL BE FOUR EXEMPTIONS ON NH&SWF CONTRIBUTIONS – RESIDENCE ONLY

1. The whole household earnings are less than $2,000 per month.
2. 65-years-old male or 60-year-old female living with their dependants.
3. House on mortgage.
4. Houses that are under $40,000 in value.

TRADING/EARNING FROM OWN PREMISES

This is for citizens who trade or provide services from their own shops/offices/depots/warehouses/stalls/factories/malls etc. and do not pay rent.

They will be entitled to contribute to the National Housing & Social Welfare Fund scheme at 20% of their premises' rent value.

The rent rate will be calculated per square feet or metre of the premises according to their location. Proper charts will be made for reference.

The property owner will have to fill in the following:

PLOT NUMBER:
DEED NUMBER:
STREET NAME:
LOCATION OF CONSTITUENCY:
CITY RATES REF NUMBER:
WATER ACCOUNT NUMBER:
SQUARE FEET/ METRES OF AREA:
PREVAILING RENT:

These will bring in contributions for the worthy cause of helping the under privileged mud and thatched huts dwellers, and for those villagers who must walk long distances to fetch a bucket of clean water.

The contributions to the NH&SWF are not tax claimable.

RENTS – RECEIVEABLE

Landlords (persons who own properties) will be categorised into the RENTAL INCOME tax category SPIT-RENTAL #

Rental income will be in the tax category SPIT/Rental or SPIT-RENT # @ 15%, which will be tax claimable.

CONTRIBUTION BY THE LANDLORD TOWARDS NH&SWF

20% of the rental will be contributed to NH&SWF which are non tax claimable.

The person/company renting the property will have to fill in a special form and will have to submit it to the Income Tax Department. This form is called: RENTAL PAYMENT FOR RESIDENCE/ COMMERCIAL PROPERTY.

The following must be filled:

TYPE OF RESIDENCE/COMMERCIAL:
PLOT NUMBER:
STREET NAME:
LOCATION:
CITY RATES REF NUMBER:
WATER ACCOUNT NUMBER:
FOR COMMERCIAL: SQUARE FEET/METRE AREA:
RENT PER MONTH:
LANDLORDS C-18 NUMBER/ TAX NUMBER/ LICENCE NUMBER:
LANDLORD'S NAME AND ADDRESS:
CONTACT NUMBERS:

This is also to be entered in the C-18 Page 2 on the rented residence or commercial section.

The rental association will make recommendations on the prevailing rentals according to the areas and localities, and will submit their report to the Income Tax Department and also to the NH&SWF for their approval and for their records.

The Income Tax Department will be linked with the Rental Association.

Rental income is classified and has its own tax category: Self Provisional Income Tax/Rentals #. or SPIT-RENTS #.

This is a straight 15% tax on the landlord when receiving rent. SPIT-RENT # receipts will be for rent paid. No other receipts will be allowed.

This will be a dual SPIT-RENT # receipt. The top part will be for the Landlord's contributions of 20% to the NH&SWF of the rent. The bottom part will be for Proprietors who will pay SPIT 15% on NET rent.

RENTAL ASSOCIATIONS

Residential or commercial property owners will have to be members of the rental association in their district.

The rental association will have records of all rented properties and will liaise with the Income Tax Department and the NH&SWF.

The records will contain the following information:

1. Description of property – code
2. Area in square feet or square metres
3. Location or area
4. Street or road/area name
5. Plot number
6. Title deed number

7. City rates reference number
8. Landlords C-18 number
9. SPIT-RENT # licence number
10. Contact number
11. Name and address
12. Rent per month

Please refer to the chart for property type code on Page 48.

ASSOCIATION

Towns/cities/districts will have a rental association whose members will be citizens who own properties and are getting rent from them.

Association members may discuss any subject matter relating to their interest and pass resolutions and so forth.

Associations must have a guidebook for reference on rentals, and annual increments or as per the lease agreements on rent (in percentages).

INCOME TAX DEPARTMENT

The regional Income Tax Office will pass on the information to the Rental Association of the constituency.

LANDLORDS' CONTRIBUTION TO NH&SWF

Landlords will have to contribute 20% of the rental to NH&SWF.

Landlords (property owners) will compulsorily have to be an association member and must have a tax category.

Any problem that the member has must be discussed in the monthly or quarterly meetings.

NH&SWF

The NH&SWF regulations on rental rates of town flats will apply, which will be 20% of prevailing rent in the area.

THE MECHANISM OF COLLECTING PROVISIONALINCOME TAX

PROVISIONAL TAX INTRODUCTION

Everybody earns a living by doing something. Some provide services, others are in business, some earn their living by being sportsmen or entertainers and some are in employment, whilst some are professionals, some are freelance. The list is long.

The earnings of each person are different, and also vary in each field of occupation, profession, business or whatever their source of income.

For this reason, 20 different tax categories have been created to clearly identify the occupation and earnings of each individual in this new system.

In the present environment in developing countries, many citizens do not pay taxes appropriately, and the rest avoid paying taxes. Therefore, all citizens from the age of 18 years will be linked to the Income Tax Department through Form C-18.

The spirit that is required in any country that wants to develop, achieve economic growth, be self-reliant and attain prosperity, is to prevent corruption in every area, be transparent and, most of all, be accountable.

With this aim, a new tax collecting system has been created. A system that is simple, practically workable and easy to administer. It is called 'The Ultimate Solution on Corruption and Tax Avoidance: A Unique System of Governance'.

This unique system will:

- Tax all those who are earning.
- Tax those who do not keep accounts.
- Cover all tax sectors of earnings.
- Create cash flow.
- Give accurate statistics.
- Allow transparency.
- Display accountability.
- Detect corruption in the early stages.
- Link all earners to the Income Tax Department.
- Identify corrupt officials.
- Provide evidence for court cases.
- Wipe out the 'Black Economy'.
- Prevent workers' strikes.
- Provide free housing for the poor.
- Prevent vote rigging.
- Prevent corruption.

THE MECHANISM OF PROVISIONAL INCOME TAX

The aim of the system is to tax ALL who earn.

Any person who earns will have to pay Provisional Income Tax on assumed profits.

This is not a sales tax but a Provisional Income Tax on profits, which will have to be paid monthly, upfront to collectors, or personally, monthly before the annual tax assessment. This will be explained step-by-step briefly on this page. (The whole procedure will be detailed in the separate tax categories section.)

This Provisional Taxation System will include VAT.

The Provisional Income Tax collected or paid by an individual will be paid in advance and will be accounted for in the annual Income Tax Assessment.

CONSTITUENCY

Every citizen from the age of 18 years will have to fill in Form C-18 at their constituency where they will vote and get their Vote Roll Number.

FORM C-18 INCOME TAX ASSESSMENT FOR CAPITAL GAINS TAX

The citizen will go through the assessment process by the Income Tax Department and will have to pay Capital Gains Tax and will be given Tax Clearance Certificate (TCC) when they have paid the tax. The TCC will show their capital amount.

TWENTY TAX CATEGORIES

After paying their Capital Gains Tax, the citizen will be categorised in to one of 20 Tax Categories and be given a Permanent Tax Number according to their trade, business, profession, occupation or employment status.

The Income Tax Headquarters will register them with one of the many Treasury Cashiers, which will have numbers. The Treasury Cashiers are the Income Tax collecting and transaction points.

PERMANENT TAX NUMBER

Every tax payer will be categorised according to their trade, business, profession, occupation or employment status.

They will be given a permanent number in their tax category followed by their Vote Roll Number.

There will be different Permanent Tax Numbers but with the same Vote Roll Number for the citizen who has more than one business.

In partnership – the Company Permanent Number will be given. For Income Tax purposes, each individual will first use the tax number of their company followed by their vote number.

The tax number allocated to them will be their permanent number. It will not be used again.

TREASURY CASHIER

All Treasury Cashiers offices will have numbers. Treasury Cashiers will be the collecting point for Income Tax.

The Treasury Cashiers will open files for all the tax payers of their categories instructed by the Income Tax Headquarters to collect their taxes.

The Treasury Cashier will sell the transaction vouchers.

The Treasury Cashier will issue a consent receipt to those who will want to print their own tickets.

CONSENT RECEIPT

All tax payers will have to print their own stationery such as invoices, receipts, cash sales etc.

They will have to register each book's numbers with the Treasury Cashier. The Treasury Cashierwill give a consent receipt, which will be a sticker on each book, and a separate receipt detailing all numbers registered.

If the Ticket Tax (tax payer) wants to print their own TTT they will have to register the tickets numbers with the Treasury Cashier and pay upfront or prepaid tax. The Treasury Cashierwill sell 'Revenue Numbered Tax Stamps' to validate the sale of second-hand items worth over $250.

The Treasury Cashierwill sell 'Numbered Daily Sales Sheets' or DSS.

The Treasury Cashierwill collect tax for Pay as you Earn (PAYE) contracts and employees from the employer.

The Treasury Cashierwill receive ALL collections from the Daily Sales Sheets and deposit them in the bank.

THE VOUCHERS:

DSS OR DAILY SALES SHEETS

The DSS will be numbered and will be sold only from the Treasury Cashier.

On the DSS, all the Tax Categories will either enter the tax they have collected from other tax categories or self-provisional tax from themselves, according to their tax rates. All the monies collected must be submitted to the Treasury Cashierevery day, week or month. The last day to submit will be ten days after the month end. For example, the January DSS deadline will be 10th February.

If the DSS are not submitted on the deadline, penalties will apply.

NUMBERED TAX REVENUE STAMPS

The Numbered Tax Revenue Stamps (NTRS) will be used to validate the purchase of second-hand items from $250.

The NTRS and Forms can only be bought from the Treasury Cashier.

TICKET TAX – TICKETS

Ticket Tax – Tickets will have to be printed by the concerned tax payer.

Each book number will have to be registered and a sticker consent receipt obtained for it from the Treasury Cashier.

Ticket Tax Tickets are prepaid tax tickets.

INVOICE

The invoice will have to be printed by the concerned tax payer. The invoice numbers must be registered at the Treasury Cashierand a consent receipt obtained for each one.

When the goods are given on account [credit], even then the provisional tax must be collected from tax payers according to their tax category through PIT-C Receipt.

RECEIPT – PROVISIONAL INCOME TAX

There will be two types of special receipts.

1. PIT-C or Provisional Income Tax – Collector receipt.
2. SPIT-## Self Provisional Receipt – Pro 1 [Accountants]
    In these receipts, it will be compulsory to write the Tax Card Number of the customer along with the invoice or cash sale number.
    The receipt will contain the Collector's or Self Collector's full details.
    One PIT-C or SPIT receipt for one cash sale or invoice number only.
3. SPIT-NC – NATURE COMMODITY [Dual Receipt]
    This is self-tax and the second part in the same receipt they will collect from the seller, usually the exempts, self-sufficient farmers, etc.

RENT RECEIPT WITH NH&SWF RECEIPT

1. The landlord will issue to the tenant the SPIT-RENT # receipt @ 20% on the top part of the receipt and;
2. On the bottom part will collect a contribution from the Proprietor @ 15% for the NH&SWF.

ACKNOWLEDGEMENT RECEIPT

The Treasury Cashierwill give an acknowledgement receipt for all the DSS received and the amount.

REGULATIONS WILL APPLY

These are the 43 regulations, which must be brought into legislation.

1. Licence
2. Registering business names
3. Tax number
4. Treasury cashier
5. Current bank account
6. Bookkeeping/accounting
7. Employers'/PAYE contracts
8. Government procurements of goods and services
9. Privatised government, parastatals, franchise holdings
10. No accounting required
11. 25% Share to all employees after tax
12. Industry
13. Form 13 – Accidental loss or act of God
14. Late submission of accounts
15. Associations
16. Tax Clearance Certificate

17. Will/inheritance/probate/executors
18. Bankruptcy
19. Amnesty
20. 20% tax theory
21. Gifts
22. Revaluation of assets
23. Tax evading penalties
24. Changing of constituency
25. Retailers
26. Trademark brands
27. Exports
28. Contractors
29. Partners
30. C-18 Vote/Tax Card
31. Religious and charity imports
32. Control on expenses
33. Foreign aid and loans
34. Price controlled items
35. Depreciation/appreciations
36. Tax concessions for over 65-years old
37. Imports
38. Capital Gains Tax
39. Renewal of C-18 form every five years
40. Civil servants
41. Residents' MP
42. Submitting stock inventories with tax returns
43. Free education, health care and subsidy on agriculture products for tax exempts

HOW THE SYSTEM WILL FUNCTION

TWENTY PERCENT TAX RATE

Every business, professionals, service providers have different profit margins. Therefore, their Provisional Income Tax will be calculated at 20 percent.

Twenty is the fifth part of hundred; so, supposing the wholesaler's profit margin is 15 percent. Now to find out the tax rate of the wholesaler: 15 divided by 5 equals 3. Therefore, 3 percent will be the wholesaler tax rate.

All the gross profit margins are in brackets.

[1] PROVISIONAL INCOME TAX COLLECTORS

Will collect:

1] Customs
2] Bank 5% from Exporters
3] Industry 5% [25%]
4] Franchise 6% [30%]

5] Wholesalers 3% [15%]
6] Retailers 4% [20%]
7] Special Imports: 4% [20%] [Health] [Education] [Agriculture] [Religion/Charity]
8] Gambling wins 10%
10] Customs – Unregulated imports 20% [Airport] [Borders]
100] Customs Retailer – Importer [8%]

REGULATIONS

Regulation 37 will apply. Please refer to page 186.

VOUCHERS

1. The Customs Department will provisionally tax according to their tax rate.
2. The Customs will issue a PIT-C1 receipt, indicating the payer's Tax number or Licence number.
3. The Customs will enter the PIT-C amount collected in the DSS.
4. The Treasury Cashierwill issue acknowledgement receipt when they receive the DSS.

PIT-C2 INDUSTRY

REGULATIONS

Regulations 1 to 7
Regulation 8 [for government procurements]
Regulation 12 [industry]
Regulations 14, 35, 37, 42

VOUCHERS

1. The industry will first raise an Invoice or a Cash Sale.
2. For each Invoice Number or Cash Sale Number they will issue a PIT-C2 receipt.
3. The industry will issue a PIT-C2 receipt, indicating the payer's Tax Number.
4. The industry will enter all the PIT-C2 receipts in the DSS.
5. The Treasury Cashierwill issue an acknowledgement receipt upon receiving the DSS.

PIT-C3 WHOLESALER 3% [15%]

Who will collect tax from whom?

Wholesalers/franchise distributors will collect mainly from licenced retailers, rural district retailers, hawkers, bars, gas stations etc., at their base tax rate or from the PIT-P [Provisional Income-Tax Payer]

Regulations

1 to 7
8 Government procurements
9, 26, Franchise holder
14, 16, 42

How will they collect Provisional Income Tax?

PIT-C 3 will issue a Cash Sale or Invoice which will have a number. They will have to write or type the customer tax number on each Cash Sale or Invoice and then issue a PIT-C 3 Receipt. The PIT-C receipt will be issued separately for each Cash Sale or Invoice number. The customer tax number is compulsory.

How are they going to record the collected tax?

PIT-C 3 will enter all their collections in the DSS form and submit them to the Treasury Cashierevery day, weekly or monthly. The Treasury Cashierwill give them an Acknowledgement Receipt.

PIT-C5 – FINANCIAL INSTITUTIONS [BANKS] 20%

PIT-C6 – COMPANIES ON THE STOCK EXCHANGE 20%

Who will collect tax from whom?

The PIT-C5 Banks and PIT-C6 Companies on Stock Exchange, upon payment of interest or dividends will issue a PIT-C receipt and deduct 20% from it.

Regulations
5, 6

How will they collect Provisional Income Tax?

PIT-C5 Banks and PIT-C6 Company on Stock Exchange will issue receipts and deduct 20% from the total interest paid or dividends.

How will the Bank and the Company remit the collected tax?

They will record all the PIT-C receipts in the DSS and remit to the Treasury Cashier.
The Treasury Cashierwill issue an Acknowledgement Receipt.

PIT-C4: FRANCHISE IMPORTERS TAX RATE 6%

Franchises are sole registered trade mark distributors of branded imported goods.
The company can locally register their trade mark brand and they will be classified as Franchise Holders of the brand name.
A company importing internationally registered trade mark brands and appointed as their distributors will be classified as a franchise.
PIT-FRNC1: [IMPORTS] Will pay to Customs 6%.
PIT-C4 FRNC: Tax Rate 6% [If they purchase from elsewhere].
RETAIL: PIT-C100 – 7% to Customs

[2] PROVISIONAL INCOME-TAX – PAYER PIT-P

PIT-P1: Licenced retailer 3% [15%]
PIT-P2: Exempt retailer 4% [20%]
PIT-P3: Bars 5% [25%]
PIT-P4: FUEL 2½% [12½%]
PIT-P6: Butchery and others 4% [20%]

NOTE: PIT-P are not allowed to collect tax.
Exempt retailers earn under $10,000 capital.

Regulations
1]Registration
2] Licence
3] Tax Category and Number
4] Treasury Cashier
5] Bank account
6] Bookkeeper
7] Employees' Certificate, 14, 23, {25}, 29, 42

Regulation
10 for PIT-P2

[3] IMPORTS – SPECIAL 20% CUSTOMS DUTY

PIT-C20: Medical
PIT-C40: Agriculture
PIT-C60: Education
PIT-C80: Religious/Charity**
PIT-100: GOVERNMENT**

NOTE: Retailers are allowed only 20% profit margin.
** No upward chain
NOTE: The Custom Duty on all PIT-C 20/40/60/80/100 are for accountability, transparency and statistics.

The concerned party will take their numbered tickets to the Treasury Cashier to be validated. The Treasury Cashierwill charge 10%, which is the Provisional Income Tax rate on each ticket. The Treasury Cashierwill give a consent receipt, which will be a stick on or written on top of the cover of each ticket book. The Treasury Cashierwill record the numbers in their register.

For one-off functions, Ticket Tax Tickets can be bought from the Treasury Cashier.
Unused tickets will be refunded.
Regulation 4 will apply.

SELF-PROVISIONAL INCOMETAX SPIT

What is Self-Provisional Income Tax?
Self-Provisional Income Tax or SPIT is a tax that the person will deduct themselves according to their tax category. They will deduct the tax according to their tax rate from their charges.

So how will the system function?
The customer with a tax number will pay for the services and get a SPIT receipt.
The SPIT payer will self-deduct the amount from the charges at their tax rate in the SPIT receipt. All SPIT receipts issued for the day will be entered into the DSS with the self-tax collected and remitted to the Treasury Cashierweekly or monthly.

The Treasury Cashierwill give them an Acknowledgement Receipt upon receiving the DSS.

Regulations
1] Business registration
2] Licence
3] Tax number
4] Treasury Cashier number
5] Bank account
6] Accountant's name
7] Employee's certificate
14] Late submissions
15] Associations
42] Submitting stocks inventory [if any]

[4] SPIT-BUSINESS – SELF PROVISIONAL INCOME TAX OR SPIT-BUS#

All businesses that are **not** in Tax Categories PIT-C or PIT-P.
These businesses are:

SPIT-BUS1:	Advertising
SPIT-BUS2;	Driving lesson schools
SPIT-BUS3:	Goods transport
SPIT-BUS4:	Hiring
SPIT-BUS5:	Sleeping places (hotels/inns/rest houses/lodges)
SPIT-BUS6:	Private hospitals/schools/boarding places
SPIT-BUS8:	Photo studios
SPIT-BUS9:	Steel works/double glazing
SPIT-BUS10:	Tyre balancing/repairs/alignment
SPIT-BUS11:	Skips/rubbish collections
SPIT-BUS12:	Carpentry/coffin boxes/furniture etc.
SPIT-BUS13:	Plumbing Contracts
SPIT-BUS14:	Electricity contractors
SPIT-BUS15:	Building/road Contracts
SPIT-BUS100:	Franchise – Retail

Note – Any other business not listed can be added from SPIT-BUS16 onwards.

Regulations: 1 to 7, 14, 42

[5] SPIT-NATURE COMMODITIES SPIT-NC# TAX RATE 10%

These SPIT-Nature Commodities are dual tax.

SPIT-NC10:	Commercial agriculture/vegetables/farmers/fruits
SPIT-NC20:	Poultry/livestock/dairy

SPIT-NC30:   Mining
SPIT-NC40:   Commercial fishing/hunting
*SPIT-NC – SECOND PART WILL BE PIT-C 100 NC.
*SELF SUFFICIENT FARMER [EXEMPT] Vote Roll Number Tax Rate 4%

Note: Nature commodities:
The SPIT-NC# receipt will be a dual receipt. It will be a double receipt if the buyer or purchaser buys from the 'self-sufficient farmer' who is in the Exempt category.

This is how the transaction will be done for 'Self-Sufficient Farmers'.
The trader in Nature Commodities, when purchasing from a 'Self-Sufficient Farmer' will issue a dual SPIT-NC# receipt on the first part and charge themselves 10% and in the second part of the receipt they will collect 4% from the seller or 'self-sufficient farmer' who is in the Exempt tax category, writing their vote roll number.

Example: The trader buys from the Self-Sufficient Farmer soya for $300. In the first part of the SPIT-NC receipt they will charge 10% [$30] to themselves and in the second part of the receipt [PIT-NC] they will collect 4% [$12] from the seller, writing their Vote Roll Number.

This is how the transactions will be done between licenced traders.
Supposing a licenced butchery shop [PIT-P6] buys a cow from the licenced farmer [SPIT-NC10] for $100. This is how the SPIT-NC10 will be issued by the farmer.

The farmer will charge himself 10%. That is $10 in the first part of the receipt [SPIT-NC10] writing the butcher's Tax Number and in the [PIT-NC] second part in the same receipt will collect 4% from the butcher that is $4. See illustration of receipt on page.....

The DSS for SPIT-NC and PIT-NC will be **dual** receipt.

[6] SPIT-PRO # PROFESSIONALS TAX RATE 10%

Professionals are those who have their own practice and employ others.

SPIT-PRO1: Accountants
SPIT-PRO2: Architects
SPIT-PRO3: Doctors
SPIT-PRO4: Lawyers
SPIT-PRO5: Opticians
SPIT-PRO6: ???

[7] SPIT-SC # SERVICE CHARGE TAX RATE 20%

Service charge where applicable.
SPIT-SC1: Banks
SPIT-SC2: Restaurants

[8] SPIT-COM # COMMISSON TAX RATE 20%*

Services working on commission.
SPIT-COM1: Insurance brokers

SPIT-COM2: Auctions
SPIT-COM3: Airline tickets sales

*20% of the commission. Supposing the agent receives 10% commission, then divide by 5 = 2% will be the tax to charge themself on the total sale.

[9] SPIT-SRV # SERVICE PROVIDERS TAX RATE 10%

Service providers.
SPIT-SRV1: Security
SPIT-SRV2: Breakdown
SPIT-SRV3: Gyms
SPIT-SRV4: Burial services
SPIT-SRV5: Garages
SPIT-SRV6: Clubs

[10] SPIT-INVS # INVESTMENT TAX RATE 20%

Investments.
SPIT-INVS1: Selling of plot
SPIT-INVS2: Buying of plot
SPIT-INVS3: Selling of property
SPIT-INVS4: Buying of property
SPIT-INVS5: Selling of bonds
SPIT-INVS6: Buying of bonds

[11] SPIT-FRANCHISE # OR GOVERNMENT PARASTATALS TAX 10%

Franchise or government parastatals which are run independently.

SPIT-GP1: Water
SPIT-GP2: Electricity
SPIT-GP3: Forestry
SPIT-GP4: Telephone
SPIT-GP5: Post Office
SPIT-GP6: Radio/Television

Note: Please refer to Regulation Number 9.
Note: In many countries the above-mentioned parastatals are owned by the government and run by NGOs. Lots of corruption is involved in it.

In other countries they are privatised with joint ownership with the government. In this way they are more efficiently run.

[12] SPIT-RENTAL # RENTALS TAX RATE 20%

Any person or company receiving rent must be registered with the following:

1. 1] The Income Tax Department – Rentals Tax Card Number
2. 2] Rental Association – Number
3. 3] National Housing and Social Welfare Funds – Contributor Number

This is a dual receipt. The landlord will issue SPIT-Rental receipt @ 15% and in the next section below the same receipt will be 20% contribution to the NH&SWF.

Note: Please see Regulation 43.

Regulations: 1, 2, 3, 4, 5, 6, 14, 15 Association, 43.

RENTAL ASSOCIATION:

The Rental Association will share an office with the NH&SWF in the district, which will keep account of all the constituencies of the district.

The Rental Association official will check all the contributions. If there is any suspicion, then it will have to be investigated.

NATIONAL HOUSING AND SOCIAL WELFARE FUNDS:

The Treasury Cashier District Office will receive NH&SWF contributions from the landlords through DSS. The Treasury Cashierwill transfer the collected amount to the NH&SWF District Office.

The NH&SWF will use the money on projects in the district.

Note: Regional NH&SWF Headquarters will also back up for any shortfalls.

[13] TICKET TAX TICKETS TTX TAX RATE 10%

A Ticket Tax Ticket will be required if the entry is by ticket.

TTX-1: All road/sea/rail
TTX-2: All entertainment/cinema/fairs
TTX-3: All sports
TTX-4: Sleeping places [if less than $10]
TTX-5: Fast Foods/restaurants
TTX-6: Self-employed*
TTX-7: Freelance*
TTX-8: Millers
TTX-9: Selling excessive livestock [Exempt]*
TTX-10: Lottery
TTX-11: All one-off events/functions*

All companies will have to print their own tickets and register the ticket numbers with the Treasury Cashier. The Treasury Cashierwill give a Treasury Cashiers Consent Receipt (TCCR) and will charge 10% tax on each ticket value. The TCCR must be stuck on each book, which will have a number to validate. The Treasury Cashierwill register the TCCR numbers.

*Ticket Tax Tickets can be bought from the Treasury Cashier

Note: Unsold tickets may be returned for refunds to the Treasury Cashier.
Note: TTX 1, 2, 3, 4, 5, 8 AND 10 **must** be registered with an association.

Regulations
1] Registration of business name
2] Licence
3] Tax Category Number
4] Treasury Cashier Number
5] Bank account
6] Bookkeeper
7] Employee display certificate

[14] P A Y E – WORK CONTRACTS:

A work contract can be defined as a fixed commitment for a certain project or assignment.

Work contracts apply mostly to actors, entertainers, sportspeople, journalists, freelancers etc.

The person entering the work contract will have to fill out a 'work contract', which will be on the company's letter head. The 'work contract' form will have to be completed by the employer or the company, which will deduct the tax and remit it. The person entering the contract will sign it.

There will be two forms. The first form will have all the personal details of the person entering the contract with their permanent employment number and the terms and conditions with the total value of the contract.

The second form will contain the personal details and the tax plan.

Please refer page 134 for full details.

[15] GOVERNMENT PROCUREMENTS OF GOODS AND SERVICES

SPIT-GOV ## TAX RATE 4% TRADERS AND CONTRACTORS
Applies to traders/contractors/service providers.
Regulation 8 will strictly apply.

TRADERS:

The traders supplying to the government will have to issue a SPIT-GOV receipt at 4% upon receiving payment. Only the licenced trader in their supply category will be able to supply with tender number.

CONTRACTORS:

Contractors will have to first finish the job according to the schedule. If it is a government contract, then the Ministry official and the MP of the constituency where the project is will inspect and sign off the finished work. If the project is by donors, then the concerned donor official will inspect and sign the finished job, together with the concerned Ministry official and the MP of the constituency before releasing payments. The contractor will have to issue SPIT-GOV receipt at 4%.

SERVICE PROVIDERS:

Licenced Service Providers will be able to provide services to the government. The service providers will issue their SPIT- ## receipt according to their tax rate when receiving payment.

RETAILERS:

Retailers are not allowed to supply to government departments.

LICENCE:

The government will issue a licence to all interested traders, contractors and service providers. The licence fee will be $1,000. All suppliers and service providers will be allowed 20% profit on their costs. They will have to issue a SPIT- receipt.

Only designated traders in specialised items of requirement will be awarded the contract.

CAUTION:

Government procurements and contracts are the key area of corruption; it must be protected with this system.

[16] GAMBLING – DUAL TAX TAX RATE 10%

PIT-C8 – Punter's win
SPIT-GMB1 – Casino's win

In gambling there is always the chance of winning or losing. Therefore, there will be two types of taxes, one for the winner (PIT-C8) and if the casino wins then it will be SPIT-GMB1. Both receipts will be issued by the gambling establishment or casino.

There will be two daily recording sections of the winning and losses in the 'DSS' or Daily Sales Sheet. One section will record the casino's gains (SPIT-GMB1) and the second section will record the casino's loses (PIT-C8). At the end of the month all the 'Casino Special DSS' will be tallied. If the casino has lost, then the losses will be recorded and will be brought forward to be deducted in another month's DSS.

If the casino has gained it will pay to the Treasury Cashier 10% of their gains as Provisional Income Tax.

Regulations:
1 Registrations
2 Licence
3 Tax number
4 Treasury Cashier
5 Bank account
6 Bookkeeper
7 Employees' certificate
14 Late submissions
15 Association

[17] NUMBERED REVENUE STAMPS SECOND-HAND ITEMS FROM $250

TAX RATE 10%

In the quest for accountability, a unique tax collection mechanism is introduced, especially for the purchase of second-hand items worth over $250.

To validate the sale, the seller will fill in two forms which, will be available from the Treasury Cashier. The forms will be titled 'Sale of Second-Hand Item'.

The seller and the purchaser name and tax numbers will be recorded on the form.

Supposing it is a sale of a car, a Toyota Corolla registration number A123456 for $2,000. The seller will go the Treasury Cashier and purchase Numbered Revenue Stamps worth $200, which is 10% of the sale value and affix it on the first form and the second form. There will be a set of two Numbered Revenue Stamps of the same number.

This is to validate the sale. All the details will be recorded. The original form will be given to the purchaser and the copy will remain with the seller.

The $50, $75 and $100 revenue stamps are numbered.

For full details of this system please refer page 130.

Illustration of the receipt is on page 133.

The main reason for these regulations and tax introduction is for deterring robbers from selling stolen items. Validating the ownership, getting tax and create transparency will make investigation easier.

[18] PAY AS YOU EARN (EMPLOYMENT) PAYE

All employment.

PAYE-CASUAL:	Use Ticket Tax Tickets
PAYE- L (Low):	From $20 to $67 (1%)
PAYE- M/L (Medium Low):	From $68 to $234 (4%)
PAYE- M (Medium):	From $235 to $499 (6 %)
PAYE- M/H (Medium High):	From $500 to $1,999 (10%)
PAYE-H (High):	From $2,000+ (20%)

* Perks, commissions, overtime, piecework, quarters to be included in final calculations before taxation.

For casual workers, the employer will give them a Ticket Tax Ticket for the amount they have earned.

All employers will compulsorily have to display the Employee's Certificate, which will indicate the name, position and the tax category of the employee.

Any person on Temporary Employment Permit (TEP) will have to follow the above table of taxation.

Note: It is very important to have a yearly 'Display Employees Certificate' because all the employees will share 25% of the employer's tax paid profit, called BONUS.*

*This is to reduce rich and poor gap.

[19] EXPORTS TAX RATE 5%

PIT-C2 – The bank will collect the provisional tax upon receiving payments from the importers.

All transactions of export will be through bank. The exporter will have to furnish all the details of the importer and their bank details.

THESE ARE THE 20 TAX CATEGORIES:

1. PIT-Collectors
2. PIT-Payers
3. PIT-Payers; special imports
4. SPIT- Business
5. SPIT – Nature commodities
6. SPIT – Professionals
7. SPIT – Service charges
8. SPIT – Commission
9. SPIT – Service providers
10. SPIT – Investments
11. SPIT – Parastatals
12. SPIT – Rentals
13. Ticket Tax
14. P A Y E – Contracts
15. SPIT – Government procurements
16. Gambling
17. Numbered revenue stamps
18. P A Y E
19. Exports
20. Exempt

[20] EXEMPT - TEMPORARY / PERMANENT VOTE CARD

The exempt will use their Vote Card as their identification.

TEMPORARY – 18 YEARS PLUS AND CAPITAL UNDER $10,000

1. Dependant male or female staying with family and have not started earning
2. Student either living in one house or in boarding and not earning
3. Rural retailers/hawkers/street vendors
4. Self-sufficient farmers

PERMANENT

1. Housewife that is not in tax categories 1 to 19
2. Disabled persons with no assets or income
3. Retired parents or elderly persons living in one house with no income or assets

Note: The self-sufficient farmer can sell their surplus to the licenced trader who will use a SPIT-NC100 receipt.

REGIONAL INCOME TAX HEADQUARTERS

The Regional Income Tax Headquarters will receive all the DSS from the Treasury Cashier Office with the deposit slips of the monthly tax collections.

The tax officials will go through each DSS and click on the account of each tax category number in the computer and will record the amount of purchases or amount paid for services and the amount of tax paid.

The Regional Income Tax Headquarterswill have precise figures of tax collections in each tax category every month.

The Regional Income Tax Headquarterswill have precise figures of each tax category payer collections every month, which will be accumulated to 12 months.

The Regional Income Tax Headquarterswill have precise figures of tax collected from each constituency and district.

The Regional Income Tax Headquarterswill also open files for the Exempt 'Self-sufficient farmers' who will sell their surplus commodities.

Vehicles and machinery will be depreciated by 10% every year. Properties will appreciate by 10% every year.

Tax payers will compulsorily submit their stock sheets with their Income Tax returns.

Penalties for late submissions will apply.

TAX EXEMPT

FROM 18 YEARS:

EXEMPT TAX CATEGORY 1
DEPENDENT – STAYING WITH FAMILY AND NOT EARNING

EXEMPT TAX CATEGORY 2
DEPENDENT/STUDYING

EXEMPT TAX CATEGORY 3
STAYING WITH FAMILY – LONG TERM SICK/DISABLED

EXEMPT TAX CATEGORY 4
DEPENDENT/OLD AGE WITH NO ASSETS

EXEMPT TAX CATEGORY 5
SELF-SUFFICIENT FARMER

EXEMPT TAX CATEGORY 6
NATIONAL HOUSING AND SOCIAL WELFARE FUNDS

EXEMPT TAX CATEGORY 7
HOUSEWIFE

TAX EXEMPT STATUS FOR 18 YEARS OLD PLUS

There are some citizens who have no permanent jobs in their constituencies. Through this system, using FormC-18, the IncomeTax Department will be able to categorise them into five different categories of tax exempts in the constituency. Total numbers of exempts in the district will be in the statistics. Through statistics, the government will be able to plan jobs. Statistics will also be useful when there is a natural disaster or to distribute emergency supplies in lean times or famine.

These are the tax exempts:

1. Housewife – no assets.
2. Student – no assets [temporary].
3. Unemployed [temporary].
4. Disabled – no assets.
5. Old age and dependant with no assets.
6. Self-Sufficient Farmer – who do not sell their commodities beyond $5,000.

The dependent student will be on temporary tax exempt, but when they start work they will have to register with the Income Tax Department in tax category PAYE.

The sick and disabled with no assets will be permanently tax exempted.

Old people with no assets will also be given permanent tax exemption status.

Self-sufficient farmers and rural traders, hawkers or street vendors, when reaching the $10,000 capital mark, will be placed in one of the 1-19 tax categories.

All the tax exempts will get a Vote Card with a C-18 number and they will be eligible to vote.

If the tax exempt person is living in a mud or thatched hut, they will qualify for low-cost housing.

The exempt cannot purchase from the PIT-C category.

To the SPIT categories their Vote Card must be shown.

Any members of the family with a Vote Card with a C-18 number, living in one house, can be used to seek services.

The tax exempts are entitled to free Education, Health Care and Agriculture Subsidies.

TAX EXEMPTIONS/TEMPORARY TAX EXEMPTIONS

TEMPORARY TAX EXEMPTION

Dependent persons staying with the family in one house and not earning.

Dependent persons staying with the family in one house and studying.

PERMANENT TAX EXEMPTION

Dependent persons staying with the family in one house and the long-term sick/disabled with no assets.

Dependent persons staying with the family in one house but of old age or retired with no assets.

SELF-SUFFICIENT FARMER

A self-sufficient farmer living in a rural village and earning enough to feed their family will be temporarily tax exempted.

They will also be eligible for subsidised fertilisers according to their quotas or land size.

The aim is to boost self-sufficient farmers to reach above the $10,000 ceiling and enable them to be listed in the tax category of Nature Commodities.

Self-sufficient farmers can also sell their surplus farm produce or livestock to the commercial sector and ask them to issue a dual receipt SPIT-NC100 receipt where the buyer will issue SPIT receipt @ 10% and also collect 4% PIT-C from the seller [self-sufficient farmer] on the value of the amount.

EXEMPT: FREE MEDICAL

The constituency office will have a medical report [see page 80] of the person and will send it to the district office to open a file.

If the exempt person needs treatment or hospital admittance, it will be free and medicines will be prescribed and obtained from a private pharmacy, which will be allowed by the government. The private pharmacy and laboratory will write down the Vote Roll number of the citizen and claim it from the government.

Note: This is a very big corruption area where medical officials from the top to bottom are involved and there are virtually no medicines in the hospitals.

EXEMPT: EDUCATION

The constituency will have data of pupils for nursery, primary and secondary and it will be free.

PROVISIONAL INCOME TAX COLLECTOR (PIT-C)

FORM C-18 PAGE 3. INCOMETAX DEPARTMENT

Q1: WHAT IS A PROVISIONAL TAX COLLECTOR OR PIT-C?

Provisional Tax Collector or PIT-C is the trade group that will collect tax in advance or provisionally on behalf of the Income Tax Department. Separate PIT-C receipts will be issued to customers and the amount of tax will not be included in the sales voucher.

A provisional tax receipt is also known as a PIT-C.

PROVISIONAL INCOMETAX – COLLECTORS PIT-C

PIT-C1: Customs – Imports 6%

PIT-C2: Banks – Exports 5%

PIT-C3: Industry – 5% [15%]

PIT-C4: Franchise/Trade Mark Brands/Agents – 6%

PIT-C5: Wholesalers – 3% [15%]

PIT-C8: Gambling [Wins]– 10%

PIT-C9: Customs – Special Imports – 4%

PIT-C10: Customs – Retailer Importer – 8%

PIT-C11: Customs – Unregulated Imports – 20%

PIT-C-EX [Cross-border Exports] – 5% SPIT – All categories 5%

Q2: WILL THEY (THE GROUP) PAY PROVISIONAL INCOME TAX AND TO WHOM?

The group will collect tax according to their tax rate from PIT-C3 to 5 Customs will collect Provisional Income Tax from PIT-C1, 9, 10 and 11.

Q3: WHAT IS UNIQUE ABOUT THIS SYSTEM?

The unique thing about this system is that for every purchase, the Tax Card Number will have to be written on the sales voucher and on the provisional tax receipt the PIT-C will have to be issued for each cash sale and invoice number. One cash sale or invoice voucher number for one PIT-C Receipt.

Tax avoidance detection (1)

The Tax Card Number will have to be recorded in the sales voucher/PIT-C Receipt and the DSS. The Income Tax Department will record every transaction through the DSS. If the trader indulges in the black economy, their purchases and sales will be matched during the year's tax assessments, which will show an imbalance. The sales should be at least 15% higher than the total purchases, if not then this must be investigated.

REGULATIONS PERTAINING TO PIT-C CATEGORY

Regulation 1: Licence will be required.
Regulation 2: Business name will have to be registered.
Regulation 3: Tax category and number will have to be obtained.
Regulation 4: To have a Treasury Cashier's allocation and number.
Regulation 5: To have a current bank account.
Regulation 6: To appoint an accountant.
Regulation 7: Employer's certificate from the Ministry of Employment.
Regulation 8: Licence (separate) if supplying to the government.
Regulation 9: Franchise of any registered trade mark or brands.
Regulation 36: Submitting stock inventories with the balance sheet.

Q4: HOW WILL THE SYSTEM WORK?

Let us take this example: Licenced retailer by the trade name of East Park Retailer buys goods from Leicester Cash & Carry (Wholesalers). The goods are worth $1,000. East Park Retailer is in Tax Category PIT-P2 and tax rate 4%.

The Leicester C&C being the Provisional Tax Collector will issue a sales voucher for $1,000, Number 123.

Then Leicester C&C will issue PIT-C5 Receipt Number A56 for $40 to East Park Retailers. This will be the advance tax collected on their behalf.

Leicester C&C will enter Number A56 in the Daily Sales Sheet. The SalesVoucher Number 123 and the PIT-P2 Licence Number and the amount collected $40 will have to be entered in a single line of the DSS. One PIT-C5 Receipt Number will have to be issued for one Sales Voucher Number 123.

The Leicester C&C will have many DSS forms at the end of the month. All the DSS amount of provisional tax collected will be added up to bring in the grand total. This amount will be handed over to the Treasury Cashier or the District Tax Office. This is the tax collected for the month.

The Income Tax Department or their district office will issue an acknowledgement receipt for the amount of DSS received for the month.

Assumed profit margins average on the listed PIT-Collectors

All trades have different profit margins and the working will be based on the assumed profit margin average in percentages.

PIT-C3:   Industry – 20%
PIT-C4:   Franchise/Trade Mark Brands – 30%
PIT-C5:   Wholesalers – 15%

As we can see, the assumed profit margins on every section are different and, therefore, to tax appropriately on each section there will be a need to adopt or find a central percentage figure to tax in all tax categories as per their earnings (profits mark-up average).

Many countries around the world have tax in four stages: that is 10%/20%/30%.40%. Therefore, this system will adopt the central figure of 20% for Provisional Income Tax calculations. The adjustment of either refunds or topping up will be done during annual tax assessments.

20% will be the Provisional Tax Collection. All the provisional tax workout will be based on gross profits. If the tax payer has paid more or less, it will be calculated and adjusted during the annual tax assessment.

20 is a fifth part of 100. Therefore, all assumed profit margins will be divided by five to be their tax percentage ratings.

Tax ratings on the PIT-C trade sections 1 to 10:

PIT-C: ASSUMED PROFIT MARGIN (DIVIDE BY 5) 20% TAX RATING

PIT-C1: CUSTOMS (Imports) 30% – 5-6%
PIT-C2: INDUSTRY 20% – 5-5%
PIT-C3: WHOLESALE 15% – 5-3%
PIT-C4: TRADEMARKS 25% – 5-5%
PIT-C6: INTEREST PAY *1) Straight 20%
PIT-C7: DIVIDENDS *2) Straight 20%
PIT-C8: GAMBLING WIN *3) (Ref regulation) 10%
PIT-C9: ROYALTIES 20%
PIT-C10: INSURANCE PAYOUTS Straight 20%

Interest paid out by the banks. Banks will issue a PIT-C6 Receipt for the amount paid and will deduct 20% of the customer's money as Provisional IncomeTax, paid off on their behalf.

Dividend payouts by companies. Companies will pay dividends by issuing the PIT-C7 receipt where they will deduct 20% as a Provisional Income Tax for their shareholders.

Gambling is a double tax category. This tax category PIT-C8 will be used for paying out the winnings. The winner will be issued with a PIT-C8 Receipt and their 10% will be deducted as a tax. There is regulation on the SPIT-Gambling tax category; please refer to SPIT-GMB 1, which is the second tax of casinos gains.

Tax paid on receipt PIT-C8 is not tax claimable (because it is not a business expense), but receipts must be kept as a proof of any jackpot wins in case the person is suspected of illegal gains or being in sudden wealth. This will also be for heavy losses, which might be the cause of bankruptcy. The receipts can be the proof.

The mechanisms of provisional taxation are detailed in the following pages.

PROVISIONAL INCOMETAX – TREASURY CASHIER

All the classes of the PIT-C category will have completed the required procedures of Regulations 1 to 9 and, in the process, they will also have been registered with the Treasury Cashier.

Treasury Cashiers are the government's agencies/agents receiving and paying offices in all districts throughout the country. Treasury Cashiers will play a big role in this system as the TC (as we will now call it) will be the centre of all dealings.

The TC will sell all the tax category's receipt books, ticket tax books, Daily Sales Sheets (DSS) and will also register all tax payers in all tax categories on the Income Tax Offices' instructions for receiving money. In the example of the transaction between the East Park Retailers and the Leicester Cash & Carry (wholesalers), we came across some alien words or sentences like: 1) C-18 Tax Number; 2) Sales Vouchers; 3) PIT-C Receipts; 4) DSS; 5) Acknowledgement Receipt. What are they?

THE TAX CARD NUMBER

The first rule of this system is that for all purchases the Tax Number of different tax categories will have to be shown and recorded in all sales vouchers. Without the Tax Card Number, no purchasing can be done. The Tax Card must be shown for any purchases to the PIT-C Tax Category and be recorded in Sales Vouchers.

SALES VOUCHERS

The second rule is that Sales Vouchers will have to be issued bearing the Tax Card's Number. The cash sale voucher will be of a special type, which will have the following details:

Seller's registered name
Voucher Number
Address
Tax Card Number
Licence Number [not compulsory]
Allocated Treasury Cashier's number.
The customer details that will be required will be as follows:
Date
Customer's name or company name
Tax Card Number
DSS Number
Line Number of DSS.
Treasury Cashier's consent receipt number on self-printed cash sales books.

(See illustration of the new type cash sale voucher on page 91)

THE PIT-C RECEIPT

The third rule is that a special receipt called a PIT-C Receipt will have to be issued on the tax rate of the customer for each Sales Voucher Number. This receipt is for the Provisional Tax collected on behalf of the customer.
One PIT-C Receipt for one Cash Sale or Invoice Voucher Number.
See illustration on page 92.
These are the details that will be required on each PIT-C Receipt:

Collector's PIT-C code (i.e., 1,2,3 to 10) Tax Number
Receipt Number
Date
Registered name and address of the collector
Collector's Licence Number
TC Number
Customer's name or company name
Customer's Licence Number
Customer's Tax Number
DSS Number and Line Number

TCCR Number
Voucher Number
Value of the voucher
Customer's tax category
Percentage rate of the customer
Tax collected

THE DAILY SALES SHEET

The fourth requirement in this system is the DSS or the Daily Sales Sheet.

This is the A4-size sheet of paper where all the daily sales transactions through cash sales, invoice or debit notes will be recorded. The sheet will contain 20 lines and on each line only one Sales Voucher Number must be entered. The DSS can only be bought from Treasury Cashiers or the District Tax Office. All DSS sheets will have numbers and will be recorded when sold to the prospective tax payer.

The DSS will record the following on each line: the date, Voucher Number, Customer's Tax Number, the amount on the Sales Voucher, the tax rate of the customer and tax collected. Behind the DSS sheet will be three lines for credit note amounts, which will be deducted from the total of the sales amount, bringing the net amount of tax collected on that DSS Number (sheet). All the DSSs must be added up for the month and submitted to Treasury Cashiers or the District Tax Office with the amount of the Provisional Tax collected. See illustration on page 93.

ACKNOWLEDGEMENT RECEIPT FROM TREASURY CASHIERS

Treasury Cashiers will issue an acknowledgement receipt to the tax payer who has submitted the DSS forms with the Provisional Tax collected in total. The Acknowledgement Receipt will mean that the tax payer is cleared from any query or investigation for that month. See illustration on page 94.

Tax avoidance detection (2)

The showing and recording of the Category Tax Card Number for all purchases plus the Sales Voucher, the PIT-C Receipt and finally submitting all DSS forms with the Provisional Tax amount results in a tight and foolproof plan of tax avoidance. If traders indulge in black economy tactics, they will be detected when their purchases through their supplier's DSS are added to show the actual amount. There will be immediate detection if anything is not in order.

These will be the basic requirements from the PIT-C group.

TAX EXEMPT BUYERS

The Tax Exempts buyers can only purchase from the retail outlets.

INCOME TAX HEADQUARTERS

The Regional Income Tax Headquarters will have separate District Offices at Tax Headquarters. There will be Regional Income Tax Headquarters at convenient locations to cater for the number of district constituencies in a large country.

The DSS will arrive from the Treasury Cashiers and distributed into respective District Offices for recording in their individual files or in computers, as per their Tax Category Card Number.

If the non-licenced retailer purchase reaches $100,000 in the year, then the Tax Exempt person will be placed in the PIT-P2 Tax Category and will have to follow procedures.

TAX CLEARANCE CERTIFICATE

After all the formalities of the Form C-18 are completed and the person is placed in one of the 20 Tax Categories, the person will receive a Tax Clearance Certificate (TCC).

The TCC will signify that the person has sorted out all taxes due. The individual's capital will be written on the TCC. This will have to be shown in certain dealings. This measure has been taken to counter tax cheats, corrupt officials, unscrupulous traders or robbers from buying or depositing monies of more than they are worth in the TCC.

Tax Avoidance Detection (3)

In the present corrupt environment of developing countries, people can deposit large sums of money in banks, can buy or build expensive houses, buy cars, jewellery and illegally send monies abroad. The introduction of the TCC will put a stop to all these illegal activities.

PRICE CONTROL ON ESSENTIAL ITEMS

The PIT-C Group, being the main trade group, will have to adhere on some essential items which are price controlled. These are: all health products and medicines, all educational materials, books and stationery, and agricultural machines, tools and commodities.

CONSENT RECEIPT FOR SELF-PRINTED BOOKS

The system will allow traders to print their own cash sale, invoice, debit note, credit note, delivery book, PIT-C receipts, SPIT-receipts, Ticket Tax books.

To validate the numbers on the books, a Consent Receipt must be obtained from Treasury Cashiers for each type of book and the total number of vouchers.

The Treasury Cashier will record the number of each book in the registrar book and issue a separate Consent Receipt for each book citing the numbers of the book on it.

The tax payer will write the Consent Receipt number on top cover of the voucher book.

The Treasury Cashier will have a separate file of each tax payer. All transactions will be recorded in it.

TREASURY CASHIER'S DEPARTMENT

THE RECORDING OF THE TREASURY CASHIER'S CONSENT RECEIPT

1. Every tax category will be allowed to print their own Sales Vouchers, like Cash Sales, Invoices, Debit Notes and Credit Notes.

    The PIT-C, SPIT- receipts and tickets will also be allowed to be printed by any tax category.

2. To validate the numbers of each sales voucher, receipt or ticket it will be necessary to be registered at the Treasury Cashier.
3. The Treasury Cashier will give a Consent Receipt Number for each type of Sales Voucher or receipt from the first number to the last number for each book.
4. The Consent Receipt Number will have to be written on the top cover of each book.
5. Any tax category using sales vouchers, receipts or tickets without a Consent Number will be penalised.
      The first thing that the inspector will look for will be the Consent Receipt Number on their random checks on every voucher book of the tax payer.
6. The charge for the Consent Receipt will be 1 cent per voucher.

THIS IS HOW THE TC RECORD CARD WILL LOOK LIKE:

TC RECORD CARD FROM PAGE 90

THIS IS HOW THE TREASURY CASHIER'S CONSENT RECEIPT WILL LOOK LIKE:

CONSENT RECEIPT FROM PAGE 90.

Tax Avoidance Detection (4)

The Consent Receipt is imposed on the traders so that they may not use other Sales Vouchers other than those numbers registered with the Treasury Cashier. The Income Tax Inspectors will first look at the Consent Receipt to see if they match the Sales Vouchers.

ILLUSTRATION: THE SALES VOUCHERS:

CASH-SALES / INVOICES / DEBIT-NOTES

Numbers 1 to 7 and 13 can be printed on the vouchers.
Numbers 8 to 12 and 14 to 18 must be written on the day of the transaction.
Purchases on credit terms will be issued with an invoice.
The PIT-C Receipt will be issued on the date of the invoice and collection.
The invoice and PIT-C Receipt can be issued after seven days of delivery.
The PIT-C Receipt must be entered in the DSS.

Illustration of PIT-C Receipts.
PIT-C RECEIPT FROM PAGE 92.

EXPLANATION OF THE PROVISIONAL INCOME TAX RECEIPTS

LINE 1:   PIT-C Tax Category. PIT-C Number. Date.
LINE 2:   All the details of seller.
LINE 3:   Customer's name, Licence Number and C-18 Number.

LINE 4:   DSS Number and Line Number, Treasury Cashier's Consent Receipt Number.

LINE 5:   Voucher Number. Value of the voucher. Purchaser's C-18 Number if the tax rate is 10%, the third line must not be used. Tax Category of the customer, their tax rate and tax paid.

NOTE – Provisional Income Tax Collectors may print their own PIT-C Receipts but will have to register the ticket numbers with the Treasury Cashier and obtain a Treasury Cashier's Consent Receipt Number.

NOTE – The PIT-C Receipt will not be valid without a TCCR number.

IMPORTANT NOTE: If the customer is from another country, then a SPIT-EXPORT Receipt must be issued @ 4%. The customer's name, country and passport number must be written. The same will be written on the DSS.

Tax Avoidance Prevention.

When the purchase is made on credit (Invoice) the tax must be collected upfront on the value of the invoice. This is to prevent fraud, tax avoidance or any misappropriation of documents.

PROVISIONALINCOME TAX - PAYER (PIT-P)

This tax category is simple and straightforward. All licenced retailers with capital of above $10,000 will have do accounting. That is recording the purchases, sales, expenses and the taxes paid in the ledgers. Annual tax assessment is compulsory for them.

Retailers are to sell their merchandise to consumers only.

Those inTax Category PIT-P are not allowed to collect any taxes.

There are two groups at present – the first group consists of proper registered licence holders who do accounting.

The second group consists of non-licenced retailers who are under the $10,000 capital threshold. The non-licenced rural retailers, hawkers or street vendors will have to obtain PIT-P3 Tax Number to purchase from PIT-Collectors and file their vouchers and do no accounting.

It is for the second type that this system has been created. There are hundreds of them in developing countries who purchase goods from wholesalers and sell them on the streets or anywhere in the present times without paying taxes.

If the non-licenced traders were to be taxed, the tax raised would match the tax raised from tax payers and that would amount to millions of dollars of extra revenue for the country.

This system will change all that. Though the system will not be able to make small traders do the accounting, this system will do the accounting for them and will keep an up-to-date record of their tax payments without them being bothered.

This system will tax all those who earn – Accounting or No Accounting.

PIT-P PART 1: THE ACCOUNTING/ LICENCE HOLDER(S)

PIT-P1:   Retail importers
PIT-P2:   Licenced retailers
PIT-P3:   Non-licenced retailers/hawkers/street vendors
PIT-P4:   Bars
PIT-P5:   Fuel

The profit margins (average) of tax contributors are not the same as each other. The average profit mark ups are:

PIT-P1 RETAIL IMPORTERS	40%	-5-	8%
PIT-P2 LICENCED RETAIER	15%	-5-	3%
PIT-P3 NON-LICENCED RETAILER	20%	-5-	4%

PIT-P4 BARS	25%	-5-	5%
PIT-P5 FUEL	12.5%	-5-	2.5%

To work out average assumed profit margins and the 20% tax, divide 100 by 20 = 5. Therefore, 20% is the 5th part of the 100%.

The assumed profit margin divided by five will equal the 20% tax rate.

For example: The rural retailer buys goods for $450 from the wholesaler. The wholesaler will issue a Cash Sale Voucher for $450 and a PIT-C3 receipt @ 4% (which is the tax rate of the rural retailer) for $18. The wholesaler (as a collector) will collect $18 through PIT-C#. The licenced retailer has paid $18 in advance – or provisional tax. This will be recorded at the Regional IncomeTax Office.

PIT-P Licence holders will follow regulations 1, 2, 3, 5, 6and 7.

Regulation 1:   Licence.
Regulation 2:   Registration of business name.
Regulation 3:   Tax Category and Number.
Regulation 5:   Current bank account.
Regulation 6:   Appoint accounting firm.
Regulation 7:   Employer's certificate (if employing)
Regulation 42:   Submitting stock inventories with the balance sheet.

IMPORTANT REGULATIONS

This tax category (PIT-P) is not allowed to collect tax.

Licence holders must file PIT-C and SPIT receipts.

Those in the PIT-P category with over $10,000 capital must appoint an accountant.

Licenced retailers are not allowed to supply to the government.

IMPORTANT NOTES ON RETAIL IMPORTERS

There are regulations on retail imports.

Retail importers have been placed in category PIT-P because they are the payer of customs duty and their PIT-C tax rate on imports is 8%.

THESE ARE SPECIAL IMPORTS – PRICE CONTROLLED CATEGORY:

PIT-P20:   All medical imports
PIT-P30:   All agricultural imports
PIT-P40:   All educational imports
PIT-P50:   All religious/charity imports
PIT-P60:   All government imports

The above PIT-P20-60 will pay 20% customs duty.

A maximum profit of 20% will be allowed.

Price control on PIT-P20/30/40/50/60 will be 20% profit.

If the PIT-P20-60 is misused, there will be a severe penalty on those who abuse it.-Anyone convicted in a corruption case will not be able to import for two years. Customs officials caught in the act will face charges and dismissal.

Retailers are not allowed to supply to any government departments.

Non-regulated imports [smugglers] at the border will have to pay double PIT-P @ 16% for the goods imported.

This practise of smuggling must be discouraged and stopped.

PIT-P 20-40 suppliers to government departments will require a licence.

Tax Avoidance Detection (6)

To prevent individuals indulging in non-legal supplies to government departments, the requirement of a special licence is introduced. This licence will be available to traders and contractors who will comply with the regulations of the government's procurement office.

NON-LICENCED RETAILERS

There are hundreds of hawkers who buy from wholesalers and sell on the streets or any place where they can find trade. These hawkers do not have licences and they keep no accounts. They compete with licenced shops by selling at cheaper prices. They can afford to do that because they have no overheads, no taxes to pay, no rates, no rental or other expenses related to running a business.

At the present time the person on the street can go to any wholesale shop and buy anything they want and start selling anywhere they please. The Income Tax Department has no clue about how to stop this type of unregulated trading. The tax revenue that is lost in this practice is huge. If the government starts to tax all those hawkers (and there are hundreds) the tax would amount to millions of dollars in revenue.

In Form C-18 these citizens will be listed as tax exempt because they will have stated that they are under the $10,000 capital threshold.Therefore, they will not require a retail licence but they will have to register with the IncomeTax Department. The non-licenced retailer or hawker or any street vendor will have to obtain a Non-Licence PIT-P3 Tax Number Card. This will be used for purchasing from the PIT-C Category like the wholesalers who will record their PIT-P3 Number and issue a PIT-C Receipt at the tax rate of 4%.

They won't be able to purchase from the PIT-C Category if they do not have a PIT-P3 Number Card.

Non-licenced retailers will do no bookkeeping until they reach the $100,000pa turnover mark or amass $10,000 capital.

At long last, a unique formula has been found that will tax all those who earn, even if they keep no accounts.

The system will **not** ask them to do any accounting, but this will be done for them at the Regional IncomeTax Headquarters.

The tax collected from these citizens will be proper, fair and accountable.

Revenues that will be generated from the non-licenced retailers will be enormous.

Tax Avoidance Detection(7)

If there will be **no** PIT-P3 Number Card, then the person will not be able to purchase anything from the PIT-C Category.

HOW THE SYSTEM WILL TAX UNREGULATED TRADERS WHO DO NO ACCOUNTING, DO NOT HAVE A LICENCE AND DO NOT PAY ANY TAXES:

Unregulated traders may continue doing business as usual, but in a different manner with this system.

ALL PURCHASES WILL REQUIRE A PIT-P3 NUMBER

The buyer will be required to show a PIT-P3 Number. This will be required to be written on the Sales Voucher (cashsales/invoices).

The PIT-P3 Number is compulsory as this will also have to be recorded in the DSS of the PIT-C Tax Group.

The seller/wholesaler will issue a Sales Voucher (cashsales/invoices) to the hawker with the PIT-P3 Number on it and after that the wholesaler will issue a PIT-C# Tax Receipt @ 4% and will collect the tax from the non-licenced hawkers for their profits.

Note: The non-licenced hawkers are advised to keep their vouchers/receipts to prove their purchases in the event of burglary/robbery/search by the police.

PIT-C GROUP

The wholesaler/seller will issue a Sales Voucher with a PIT-P3 Number on it and then issue a (separate) PIT-C3 Receipt @ 4%.

The wholesaler will record the sale in the DSS with the voucher number PIT-P3 Number/the amount of tax collected.

At the end of the month, they will hand over all the tax collections and the Daily Sales Sheets to the Treasury Cashier or District Tax Office.

Wholesalers or any trade/service are not allowed to issue a Sales Voucher without a PIT-C Receipt Number. Failure to issue a Sales Voucher without a PIT-C Receipt upon sales will be an offence.

The Treasury Cashier's or District Tax Office

The Treasury Cashier's Office will send the total DSS collected/received from the PIT-C group to the IncomeTax Headquarters.

IncomeTax Headquarters

Traders in the PIT-C Category will send DSS forms to the Treasury Cashier with the amount collected from PIT-P. The clerks at the Regional Income Tax Headquarters will enter all the entries from the DSS to each numbered file the amount collected for Provisional IncomeTax.

At the end of the year, the Regional Income Tax Headquarterswill know the amount collected from each PIT-P tax payer.

In this way all C-18 Numbers (exempt categories under the $10,000 threshold capital) will have to pay taxes.

All other tax categories will be taxed at their indicated tax rate. Accounting will be done for them at the IncomeTax Headquarters.

The record of PIT-P3 tax payments can be obtained every month from the District Constituency Office within the IncomeTax Headquarters upon request or for any investigation.

At the end of the financial year, the PIT-P3 tax payers will have their total tax paid figures. The PIT-P3 tax payer will be advised to obtain a trading licence if their capital reaches the $10,000 mark or their purchases reaches $100,000.

The ultimate gain for the government will be enormous, as this will bring into its fold hundreds of new tax payers, generating millions in extra tax from a tax collecting system that is not complicated but practically effective and workable.

The PIT-C and the PIT-P are the main tax categories that are directly linked with general trade.

The SPIT – all except the business category – are linked to services.

As we have noted how the Provisional IncomeTaxCollector and the Provisional IncomeTax Payer tax system works. In the same manner there is Self-Provisional Income Tax – this tax category has ten separate sections that will be recorded daily when services are provided and the SPIT-Receipt will be issued for the amount paid.

The workings will be the same, except that SPIT Category tax payers will charge themselves at the tax rate prescribed for their category. They will record their SPIT-Receipt in the DSS with a Sales or Service Voucher Number. In some SPIT Categories a receipt will suffice.

CONTROLLED PRICES ON ESSENTIAL ITEMS: HEALTH, EDUCATION, AGRICULTURE

HEALTH: Medicines, equipment, items for the disabled or any health-related items will be allowed 10% profit by PIT-C importers. The retailers will be allowed 20% profit.

EDUCATION: Text books, exercise books, papers, pens, pencils or any educational items should be sold by the importers at 10% profit to the retailers. The retailers are allowed 20% profit.

AGRICULTURE: Fertilisers, seeds, equipment or any agricultural items are allowed 20% profit by the importers.

IMPORTS CUSTOMS DUTY ON:

Health – 20%
Education – 20%
Agriculture – 20%

CONTROLLED PRICES WILL HAVE A 20% PROFIT MARK UP ON LANDED COST

For example: The wholesaler in Tax Category PIT-C3 imports fertilisers and the landed cost of the item is $20. The maximum profit allowed will be 20%, which will make the cost of selling the bag of fertiliser $24 fixed price.

If the retailer wants to buy from the wholesaler, the selling price of the fertiliser will still be the same $24. The discount the wholesaler will offer will be from their profit. However, if the retailer's shop is over 50 miles or 100 kilometres away then the transport cost with the valid SPIT-BUS# receipt can be added equally on each bag.(Supposing the transport cost is $200 for 50 bags, therefore 200 divided by 50 = $4.) The retailer will be allowed to sell at $28 per bag. If the distance is more than 100 kilometres, then five cents per kilometres can be charged on top of the $24 fixed price, per bag.

RETAIL IMPORTERS AND PRICE CONTROL

They can only sell retail.
They cannot supply to government departments if they do not have a wholesale licence.
They can supply to their branches under the same registered business name.

TAX CATEGORY SPIT

SELF-PROVISIONAL INCOMETAX

1. Professionals
2. Service Providers
3. Businesses
4. Farming/Agriculture
5. Franchise/Government Parastatals
6. Exports
7. Service Charges

10% SELF-PROVISIONAL INCOMETAX CATEGORIES

The Self-Provisional IncomeTax system dictates that individuals or companies will have to charge themselves as per the tax category according to their occupation.

Individuals or companies will tax themselves by issuing a SPIT- Receipt for services or sales rendered. The tax workings will be based on the amount of the sales/service voucher and after that the tax rate (percentage) will be applied for the tax amount. The SPIT- Receipt will be given to the customer for their tax expenses claims.

SPIT- Receipts must be recorded in the DSS on a daily basis. Sales Vouchers are compulsory and they are the cashsales or invoices.

For example:

A PIT-C3 customer [a wholesaler] comes to an accounting firm for them to do his accounts. The accounting firm is in Tax Category SPIT-PRO1.

This is how the accounting firm will record the transaction:

Firstly, they will raise an invoice for the amount agreed (that is $500) to do the accounts.

Secondly, they will issue a SPIT-PRO1 Receipt at 10% (this is their tax rate) on the $500.This is the tax that they will charge themselves and they will record the invoice and the SPIT- Receipt Number in the DSS, which will be done on daily basis. The DSS should be submitted at the end of the month with the total amount of self-collection to the Treasury Cashier with other (if any) DSS forms. An Acknowledgement Receipt should be obtained. The $50 is the Provisional Tax on the accountants. The wholesaler will be able to claim the $500 accountant's fees as a business expense in his books if he has the accountant's SPIT-PRO1 Receipt.

No business expense will be considered during tax assessment without a valid SPIT- Receipt.

Important Note: All SPIT categories must issue cash sale or invoice first and then issue a SPIT- Receipt.

The SPIT category will first raise an invoice or cash sale and then issue a SPIT- Receipt.

The IncomeTax Headquarters will record all daily collection sheets and will wait for tax returns for it to be assessed for any refunds or top ups.

It is an offence for the service or sales to be done if the Sales Voucher and SPIT- Receipt are not issued.

THE FOLLOWING SHOWS HOW THE SPIT- RECEIPT WILL LOOK:

DETAILS OF THE SELF-PROVISIONAL INCOME TAX RECEIPT:

LINE 1:
1. This is the SPIT-PRO1 Receipt.
2. Number of the SPIT-PRO1 Receipt.

LINE 2:
3. Name of company.
4. Date.
5. Allocated Treasury Cashier's Number.

LINE 3:
6. Address and contact number of company.

LINE 4:
7. Tax Category and Licence Number (AG321).
8. Tax Rate of the SPIT-PRO1.

LINE 5:
9. Customer's name.
10. Customer's Licence Number.

LINE 6:
11. Daily Sales Sheet and Line Number.
12. Treasury Cashier's Consent Receipt Number.

LINE 7:
13. C-18 Number (if the purchaser is Tax Exempt).

LINE 8:
1. Customer's Tax Category.
2. Sales Voucher Number.
3. Amount of the Sales Voucher.
4. SPIT Tax Rate of PRO1.
5. SPIT Tax.

All sales or services must have a cash sale/invoice followed by a SPIT- Receipt.

SELF-PROVISIONAL INCOME TAX (SPIT)

Exempts are not allowed to purchase from the PIT-C Category.

All other Tax Categories will be taxed at their indicated tax rate. The accounting will be done for them by the District/Constituency Office within the IncomeTax Headquarters.

The SPIT workings are similar to that of Provisional Income Tax (PIT). The difference is that they will not collect but will tax themselves. Regulations one to six are compulsory while the rest of the regulations may be applicable where necessary.

SALES OR SERVICES

A Sales Voucher will be issued for all sales or services rendered. A SPIT- Receipt must be issued.

The SPIT- Receipt must be issued upon receiving payments from the customer. The SPIT- tax payer will charge themselves the tax rate of their category.

The Sales Voucher amount and the SPIT amount will be entered in the DSS on a daily basis and in sequential order.

All DSSs will be totalled and the amount accumulated will be submitted to the Treasury Cashier at the end of the month.

INCOME TAX HEADQUARTERS

The Income Tax Headquarters will have separate District Offices.

All these offices will be in the headquarters complex.

The DSSs will be sent to their respective District Office. All details will be derived from the DSS line-to-line and will be recorded in individual files. In this way the tax payer and the exempt categories' tax pay-ins will be recorded.

The Ten Self-Provisional Tax Categories are:

Professionals
Service providers
Businesses (not in category PIT-C or PIT-P)
Nature Commodities
Investments
Suppliers to government procurement departments
Exports
Commissions
Service charges
Franchise holders

Important note:

The Sales Voucher alone will not be valid without a SPIT- Receipt.

Not issuing a Sales Voucher and SPIT- Receipt when the sales or services are rendered will entail tax evasion penalties.

PROFESSIONALS ARE THOSE WHO HAVE UNIVERSITY DEGREES/DIPLOMAS/ CERTIFICATES AND WHO RUN THEIR OWN PRACTICES AND EMPLOY OTHERS

3.	Accountants:	SPIT-PRO 1
4.	Architects:	SPIT-PRO 2
5.	Doctors:	SPIT-PRO 3
6.	Lawyers:	SPIT-PRO 4
7.	Opticians:	SPIT-PRO 5
8.	Dentists:	SPIT-PRO 6

(Add other professionals that are not on the list.)
The above list 1-6 is for Tax Category SPIT-PRO.

REGULATIONS

Licence.
Registered business name.
Tax Category and C-18 Number.
Registered at the Treasury Cashier.
Bank account number.
Annual accounting/auditing.
(If employing:) Certificate of Employees'
Association.

SERVICE PROVIDERS

This category is for all service providers.

TAX CATEGORY SPIT-SPV 10%

Health clubs/massages/SPIT-SPV1.
Clubs/SPIT-SPV2.
Debt collectors/SPIT-SPV3.
Barbers/beauticians/SPIT-SRV4.
Associations/SPIT-SRV5.

(Add other service providers that are not in the list.)
Regulations to be followed: 1-7 and 11.

ANY BUSINESSES THAT ARE NOT IN TAX CATEGORIES PIT-C AND PIT-P:

SPIT-BUSINESE Tax Rate 10%.

Contractors (all)	SPIT-BUS1.
Driving schools	SPIT-BUS2.
Goods transport	SPIT-BUS3.
Hiring (all)	SPIT-BUS4.

Sleeping places/motels	SPIT-BUS5. (Charges over $10, otherwise Ticket Tax will apply.)
Private hospitals	SPIT-BUS6.
Private schools	SPIT-BUS7.
Garages	SPIT-BUS8.
Security guards	SPIT-BUS10.

(Add here any SPIT-Business Tax Category that is not listed.)
Sleeping places under $10 come under the TicketTax Category.
SPIT-Business Tax Category will have to follow these regulations:

Licence.
Registered business name.
Tax Category and C-18 Number.
Registered at the Treasury Cashier.
Bank account number.
Annual accounting/auditing.
(If employing:) Certificate of Employees' Association.
Suppliers to government departments.*
Associations.**
Submitting stock inventories with the balance sheet (where necessary).

* A second licence is required.
** Not all of the group will be required to join an association.

NATURE COMMODITIES

SPIT-NC Tax Rate 10%:

Commercial agriculture	SPIT-NC1.
Livestock/diary/poultry	SPIT-NC2.
Farming/agriculture (both)	SPIT-NC3.
Commercial fishing/hunting	SPIT-NC4.
Mines	

Regulations 1 to 7 apply.
Regulation 8 will apply to government suppliers.
Regulation 11: Membership of associations or societies.
Regulation 42: Stock inventories to be submitted with the balance sheet.

GOVERNMENT PARASTATALS OR PRIVATISED

SPIT – PARASTATALS ## TAX RATE 10%
These are the government parastatals:

Water.
Electricity.
Telephones ground lines.

Broadband internet stations.
Televisions stations.
Radio broadcasting stations.
Mobile phone stations.
Forestry.
Mines.
Airlines.

The government may privatise the above parastatals to companies that will be called franchises.

SPIT: FRANCHISE OF PARASTATALS SPIT-FRN 1-10.

Tax rate: 10%
All the rules and regulations of the SPIT- system will apply.

EXPORTS. TAX RATE 5%

PIT- C EXP / BANK

All exporters must have a licence from the Ministry of Finance.
Please refer to the Exports chapter and Regulation 27 for full details.
Exports of all goods will be regulated and monitored by the Ministry of Finance.
All export quantities, weights and amounts should be sent to the Ministry of Finance for statistical purposes.
Exporters will be allowed to use one commercial bank only for all their transactions.
The SPIT-EXPO Receipt may be issued by the bank upon receiving payments.
The government and Chambers of Commerce will promote exports.
There will be 5% PIT–C for all exports payments received.

SERVICE CHARGES

Service charges: SPIT-SCH tax rate 20%.
All service charges will be SPIT-20% of the amount charged.
For example: The bank charges $50 to the customer for service charges; this is how it will be worked out. When charging the customer $50, the bank will issue a SPIT-SCH20 Receipt. The bank will charge 20%, meaning $10 to themselves.
The bank has paid through SPIT-SCH20 Receipt $10 towards their customer's Provisional IncomeTax.
The customer will record the $50 SPIT-SCH20 Receipt in their account books as a business expense.

SELF-PROVISIONAL INCOMETAX: 4% TAX CATEGORY SUPPLIERS TO GOVERNMENT DEPARTMENTS

GOVERNMENT PROCUREMENTS/SUPPLIERS TO THE GOVERNMENT

Suppliers to the government are profit controlled.
The maximum profit allowed on cost will be 20%.

LICENCE

Retailers will not be allowed to supply.
The licence can be obtained from the Ministry of Finance.
This is a secondary licence which will be issued based on the original trade licence.
The issuing of the licence will depend on the capital of the Tax Clearance Certificate.

SPIT-GS4: TAX RATE 4%

All suppliers to the government will have a second SPIT-GS4 Tax Category.
The SPIT-GS4 Receipt will be issued when the payment will be effected.
Suppliers will have to specify the product they will want to supply and will send a price list on 20% based on profit workout every six months.
Suppliers will share the quantity equally at the common set price if it is the same commodity/product.
If the company/supplier is caught in any corruption, the penalty fine will be ten times the value of the invoice and the licence will be cancelled if caught a second time.
Road Contractors will be awarded contract by tenders. The contract will be based on stages of work. The payment will be made after the completion and inspection of that work by the ministry concerned, the MP of the constituency and, if it is through donors, the representative will sign.
Note: This is the highest are of corruption and this system must be followed rigorously.

SELF PROVISIONAL INCOME-TAX: COMMISSION

SPIT-COMMISSION (SPIT-COM)

Self-Provisional IncomeTax on commission will vary according to the commission received.

This Tax Category includes royalties.

Those receiving commission from any quarter will be placed in the SPIT-COM Category.

The rate of tax will be based on the percentage figure, divided by five.

For example: the SPIT-COM tax payer receives 20% commission on the sale or service rendered for $400.

This is how it will be worked out: 20% of $400 is $80. Therefore, $80 is the commission received. Divide by five for the Tax Rate and the Provisional Tax will be $16. SPIT-COM20 will be worked out and the percentage of the tax must be put after the COM – which is to say, 20 divide by 5 = 4%. This is the tax rate of the 20% commission.

This is the table for SPIT-COM#:

SPIT- COM20* (20 percent) = 4%
SPIT- COM15 (15 percent) = 3%
SPIT-COM10 (10 percent) = 2%
SPIT-COM5 (5 percent) = 1%

SELF-PROVISIONALINCOMETAX: (1)INVESTMENTS (2)EXPORTS

SPIT CATEGORY: SPIT-INV# INVESTMENT(S)

TAX RATE 20%

All investments must have a Tax Clearance Certificate.
> All investments are in the SPIT-INV Category and will pay Provisional IncomeTax of 20%.
> The following are the deals that are categorised as investments:

> Sale/purchase of land or plots.
> Sale/purchase/building of commercial property.
> Sale/purchase/building of residential property.
> Sale/purchase of jewellery.
> Sale/purchase of arts or antiques*
> Sale/purchase of shares/bonds

EXPORTS: TAX CATEGORY PIT-C2 [5%]

> All exporters will require a licence, which can be obtained from the Ministry of Finance.
> All exporters are required to belong to an association/the Chambers of Commerce.
> These are the codes for PIT-C2 BANK:

> Exports of mine products
> Exports from industries
> Exports of agricultural produce
> Exports of fish or livestock
> Exports diary, poultry products
> Exports of fruits and vegetables

*Add exports items to this list.
> The bank will collect PIT-C or Provisional IncomeTax upon receipt of payments from the importers.
> Exporters are allowed to use one bank only.

TAX CATEGORY TTX - TICKETTAX

WHAT IS A TICKET TAX?

Ticket Tax is the tax paid ticket which has the Consent Number of the IncomeTax Department or their agents (Treasury Cashier) on it.

The main reason to introduce a Ticket Tax is to obtain tax from lots of minibuses and rickshaws that operate in abundance in developing countries without paying any significant taxes. The tax collected from this sector will be enormous.

Entry to all entertainments and sports will require a Ticket Tax Ticket.

The Ticket Tax Ticket can be printed by obtaining a Treasury Cashier's Consent Receipt or Ticket Tax Books purchased from the Treasury Cashier.

There are lots of cheap rest houses in developing countries which charge $10 per night or less. There is no point in registering these rest houses into a SPIT- Tax Category – rather, they should be in the Ticket Tax Category.

The Ticket Tax Category will have to be in an association. The reason for this is that they will have to be properly regulated, organised and be accountable.

In rural villages there are millers who will have to be taxed by Ticket Tax.

Freelances and self-employed people who do odd jobs will receive a Ticket Tax Ticket as a receipt by the employer. Fast food chains, takeaways or temporary food stalls must provide Ticket Tax Tickets, which can be used as vouchers. Self-sufficient farmers will use Ticket Tax Tickets to sell their excess produce or livestock.

For Ticket Tax Tickets the company or person will have to register first with the IncomeTax Department through the Treasury Cashier and have a file opened with a Permanent Ticket Tax Number. These tax paid tickets can be bought from Treasury Cashiers or can be printed by the above organisations with a Consent Number on them from the Treasury Cashier.

The process and regulations are fully explained in the following pages.

The Ticket Tax will not be valid if there is no Consent Number from the Treasury Cashier on it.

SPECIAL EVENTS/FUNCTIONS/SHOWS – TICKET TAX

The tickets may be purchased from Treasury Cashier with a Consent Receipt and permit to hold the occasion.

The tickets cannot be used for other events other than the permission granted.

Full Ticket Books may be returned [unused] and will be refunded.

If the promoters would like to issue special tickets for events, they may do so but will have to follow the procedures as shown and illustrated in the following pages.

No refund will be allowed on special tickets.

These are the categories of TicketTax:

TTX/1. All road/rail/sea/passenger travel fare.

TTX/2. All entertainment (entry by ticket).

TTX/3. All sports (entry by ticket).

TTX/4. Sleeping places – (less than $10 per night per person).

TTX/5. Freelance/self-employed.

TTX/6. Fast foods/takeaway/temporary stalls.

TTX/7. Millers.

TTX/8. Selling of excessive livestock/agriculture products.

TTX/9. Lottery (tickets).

TTX/10.*All events/functions with entry by ticket.

* This is a new tax system designed to tax events which can be organised by having a permit.   .

In this Tax Category it is not necessary to show identification or to record it.

Ticket-Tax Categories (1/2/3/4/6/9) must belong to an association.

If any of the above Tax Categories earnings are over $10,000, or turnover exceeds $100,000, Regulation 6 (annual accounting/auditing and tax assessment) will need to be followed and be removed from the Exempt Category.

TicketTax Tickets can be purchased from the Treasury Cashier in smaller amounts (5c/10c/20c/50c).

Tickets can be purchased in books:

(1) BOOK OF TICKETS (2) VALUE (3) TAX COLLECTED (4) BOOK VALUE (5) TOTAL

500 5c $2.50 $2.00 $4.50
500 10c $5 $2.00 $7.00
500 20c $10 $2.00 $12.00
100 50c $5 $2.00 $7.00

Note: The above books can be purchased from the Treasury Cashier.There is no TCCR fee. The purchase will be recorded at the Treasury Cashier on their Permanent File Number.

TCCR = Treasury Cashier's Consent Receipt.

TTX – 04 TICKET-TAX

PRINT YOUR OWN TICKETS

(1) Ticket Tax Categories 1 to 9 may print their own tickets as per their requirements, to the value of the ticket required.

For example: A football club has printed 100 books of tickets with 100 tickets in each book at the value of $6.48 per ticket, plus 60 books of tickets (100 in a book) to the value of $2.30 per ticket. The numbers of the $6.48 tickets are 001 to 10,000 and the number for the $2.30 tickets are 001 to 6000.

To validate the tickets the football club will only take the numbers of the $6.48 and $2.30 to the Treasure Cashier's Office.

The Treasury Cashier will issue a TCCR deriving the club information from their file.

The numbers of $6.48 tickets belonging to the club, the Licence Number MOS/123 and the Tax Category TTX/3 are 001 to 10,000 and the numbers of the $2.30 tickets are 001 to 6000. The Licence Number is MOS/123 and the Tax Category TTX/3.

The Treasury Cashier will issue a TCCR (Treasury Cashier Consent Receipt) for the $6.48 first.

The Treasury Cashier will calculate the 10,000 tickets @ $6.48 ($64,800.00) @ the tax rate of 10% ($6480.00).

This is what the Treasury Cashier's Consent Receipt will look like:

TTX – 05 TICKETTAX

PRINT YOUR OWN TICKETS, PART 2

The second TCCR will be issued in the same way, with the same licence details. So:

The football club's Licence Number MOS/123 in Tax Category TTX/3 will never be able to use the same numbers ever again.

Instead, they will have to begin with numbers such as 'A0001' up to 'AA999999' or 'AAA999999'. Explanation of TCCR:

1. XYZ government = Country government.
2. Ministry of Sports = This indicates that the licence was issued by the Ministry of Sports.
3. TCCR Number – JN/787. This will be picked up from the number sequence in the scroll, which will have 13 columns to record the details from 1 to 13 of the issue of the TCCR.
4. The TCCR receipt will record the month the receipt was issued. There will be two letters relating to each month:

    January = JN
    February = FB
    March = MR
    April = AP
    May = MY
    June = JU
    July = JY
    August = AU
    September = SP
    October = OT
    November = NV
    December = DC

TTX 06.TICKET-TAX

PRINT YOUR OWN TICKETS (CONT.)

1. TC = Treasury Cashier Number plus File Number.

2. Licence Number: This will be supplied by the ministry, as indicated on the top of the TCCR Receipt, below the government. In this case, it is the Ministry of Sports (MOS).
3. TTX Category = This football club is in category TTX/3.
4. Ticket Value = This is the value of the ticket, ranging from 5c to $99.00.
5. Numbers from = Starting numbers that are required to register for the TCCR.
6. Numbers to = The last number of the starting number.
7. Books = The quantity of books that will held, with the numbers indicated from No. 7 to No. 8.
8. Total tickets = This is the total number of tickets, from No. 7 to No. 8.
9. Ticket value = No. 10 multiplied by No. 6 = The ticket's value.
10. TTX 10% = This is the actual tax paid by the No. 4 Licence Holder.
11. Date = Date of the TCCR Receipt.

INSPECTION AND RANDOM CHECKS

The Ticket Tax Inspector in plain clothes will undertake random checks on the licence holders by being in the crowd. He or she will check on the numbers and value, making sure that they tally with the TCCR, and also the date of inspection and the ticket numbers to determine the usage and the approximate date of the tickets likely to finish. This will be compared from the date of purchase on average.

Note: The TCCR Number will appear on all of the books and tickets.

For information of Treasury Cashier procedure, please refer to 'Treasury Cashiers'.

The tax collected from all the contributors of the TTX Categories will be calculated individually, every month, by the Treasury Cashier and passed on to the Income Tax Headquarters to be recorded in each individual Tax Payer's File.

If profits exceed $10,000 or sales are above $100,000 annually, then the taxpayer will have to submit annual accounts and undertake auditing for tax assessment purposes and will be removed from the EXEMPT Category.

TICKETTAX/TTX REGULATIONS, AFTER ALL THE FORMALITIES OF REGISTERING ARE COMPLETE

1. The TicketTax Tickets must be given, equivalent to the fare or entrance fee.
2. For example, a bus fare is $19.35 and, this being so, the bus conductor will issue the tickets to the value of the fare, that is (1) a $10 ticket, (2) a $5 ticket, (3) four $1 tickets, (4) a 20c ticket, (5) a 10c ticket, and (6) a 5c ticket (= $19.35).
3. The bus company can print their own tickets (please refer to the details outlined in this section).
4. The TicketTax Tickets can be purchased from the Treasury Cashier in the following values: 5c, 10c, 20c, 50c, $1, $5, $10.
5. A TCCR Consent Receipt is required to validate the TicketTax Tickets.
6. The Treasury Cashier will record **all** purchases of the ticket books in the holder's file and will calculate the annual figure. The collection of tax during the year will be compared with the following year's collection to assess the progress/growth of the company.
7. The Treasury Cashier will design appropriate forms for recording the transactions in the file.

8. The TicketTax Tickets bought from the Treasury Cashier will **not** attract any **extra** fees for a TCCR.

9. The TCCR fee for the owner's printed tickets will be $1 per book of 100 tickets **or** 1 cent per ticket.

10. Companies or organisations will not be allowed to repeat the numbers on their printed tickets for ten years.

11. Permits will be required to host any sports event/put on fast food stalls/and for any events in the TTX 1-10 Category that is temporary or occasional.

12. The permit must be prominently displayed and can be obtained from the Treasury Cashier/ City Council/District Commissioner.

13. The Tax Rate on the ticket is 10% of its value.

14. The Ticket Tax Books TTX 1-10 are available from the Treasury Cashier.

TICKETTAX: ILLUSTRATION OF TICKETTAX TICKETS

Illustration 1: Road/rail/sea fare
Ministry of Transport
Tax category: TTX/1

Numbers 1/2/3/4/9 printed
Numbers 5/6/7/8 written

Note: If the holder has a licence, then there is no need to write the C-18 Number.

Illustration 2: Fast food, takeaways & food stalls
Licence from the Ministry of Health
Tax category: TTX/6

Note: If the bill is for $2.75, then Voucher 8880 is worth $2.50, and for 25c TicketTax Tickets must be used.

TICKETTAX. ILLUSTRATIONS OF TICKETTAX TICKETS

Illustration 3: Entertainment/cinemas/amusements
Ministry of Entertainment/Culture
Tax Category TTX/2

Illustration 4: All sports
Ministry of Sports
Tax Category TTX/3

TICKET TAX AVOIDANCE DETECTION:

For example, a minibus operator registered at the Treasury Cashier had been buying TTX or Ticket Tax Tickets for $1,000 per month for his one minibus operation But now buys for only $600. The downward trend must be investigated.

SELF-PROVISIONAL INCOMETAX & PIT-C8 GAMBLING

SPIT-GMB

GAMBLING

Gambling will be taxable by 10% to the winner as well as the casino.
Gambling will be covered by two tax categories:

PIT-C08:   A receipt will be issued to the winning person with a tax of 10%.
SPIT-GMB 1:   A receipt will be issued by the gambling joint or casino with a 10% tax on all gains.

There will be two daily record sheets:
One daily record sheet will record the casino's losses (PIT-08).
One daily record sheet will record the casino's gains (SPIT-GMB1).
At the end of any day or session of time, the casino will calculate all PIT-C8 and SPIT-GMB1 Receipts and subtract the higher figure from the lower figure to arrive at the calculation of the gains or losses of the day.

For example:
Three punters, X, Y and Z, go to the casino. All three buy chips/tokens to the value of $500 each.

X is issued with Sales Voucher 1001 for $500.
Y is issued with Sales Voucher 1002 for $500.
Z is issued with Sales Voucher 1003 for $500.

At the end of the day, X has $2,400 worth of chips/tokens, Y has $0, and Z has $200 worth of chips/tokens.
This is how the casino will record the Sales Vouchers:
X will be issued with a PIT-C8 Receipt ($2,400 – $500 = $1,900 @ 10% tax = $190 = tax deducted and retain Sales Voucher Number 1001.
Y does not return the Sales Voucher, indicating that he has not returned Voucher 1002. Therefore, the casino will issue (after 24 hours) a SPIT-GMB1 on absent Sales Voucher No. 1002 for $500 @ 10% = $50 Provisional IncomeTax.
Z has $200 when he returns Sales Voucher 1003. The casino issues a SPIT-GMB1 Receipt for $200 (SPIT-GMB1 gains = $300 @ 10% = $30 Provisional IncomeTax.
If punters want to cash out, they need to return the Sales Voucher to the cashier; or, if they have lost all the money, then the Sales Voucher will act as proof of their loss.

SPIT-GMB: ILLUSTRATION OF PIT-C8 AND SPIT-GMB1 RECEIPT

NUMBERED REVENUESTAMPS: SECOND-HAND ITEMS VALUED OVER $250.00

NUMBERED REVENUE STAMPS:SELLING OF SECOND-HAND ITEMS $250 AND ABOVE

Note. Please refer to Regulation 40

In the quest for accountability, a special tax collection mechanism will be introduced for purchasing second-hand items worth $250 and above.

In developing countries where there are countless robberies, recovered property is often not returned to the owners due to the difficulty in proving ownership. Any person, when they are apprehended, can show false purchase papers, and it is impossible for police to challenge the authenticity of the items due to time and costs.

In many cases, the culprit is also able to bribe the police involved in the investigation.

For these reasons, a new system is needed – and the following may be useful.

With the new system, any person who wants to sell a second-hand item worth in excess of $250 will need to purchase two forms, these titled 'Sale of Second-Hand Item', and available from the Post Office, District Tax Office, or from Treasury Cashiers.

Secondly, the seller will be required to pay a Provisional IncomeTax of 10% of the value of the item by affixing a set of two numbered Revenue Stamps on the first form and the copy. Once this has been completed, the Treasury Cashier will supply the seller with a receipt (this illustrated on page 133), which will be stapled onto the second form and retained by the seller. The stamped form given to the purchaser will then act as a validation of ownership – and, should they want to sell the item any time, they will need to repeat the above process.

Only $50, $75, $100 and $500 Revenue Stamps will be numbered.

If the seller is a taxpayer, the tax paid in buying the numbered Revenue Stamps is Provisional Tax.

If they are taxpayers, the purchaser will also need to enter the newly bought item into their purchase ledgers.

Before selling any item, the sellers will need to check the Tax Clearance Certificate, to ascertain that the purchase is within the bounds of the purchaser.

This plan should make it easier to identify any stolen property, and its rightful owners. And if someone is suspected of robbery, asking for the Sale of Second-Hand Item Form will be of use in ascertaining their guilt. It is also useful because the Tax Clearance Certificate stops people from buying things that they are not entitled to.

TREASURY CASHIER'S DEPARTMENT: SALES OF NUMBERED REVENUE STAMPS FOR SECOND-HAND ITEMS WORTH $250 OR MORE

The seller of any second-hand item worth over $250 will need to purchase numbered Revenue Stamps from a Treasury Cashier to validate the sale.

The Treasury Cashier will issue a receipt for the purchase of the set [two] of numbered Revenue Stamps with similar numbers.

The seller will pay 10% of the sale value in Provisional Tax to the Treasury Cashier and obtain a receipt, which he will attach to his copy.

Only the $50, $75, $100 and $500 Revenue Stamps will be numbered. Revenue stamps from $1 to $20 will not be numbered.

There will be two special forms for the sale of second-hand items over $250.

The first form will be affixed with the required numbered Revenue Stamps [dual numbered] in order to validate the sale.

The first form will be given to the purchaser.

The second form will remain with the seller, along with the Treasury Cashier's Receipt of 10% Provisional IncomeTax.

The Treasury Cashier will write the C-18 Number of the seller and the purchaser on the receipt, and also supply the item being sold with a registered (or serial) number.

An illustration of the Treasury Cashier Receipt can be found on page 133.

The Second-Hand Sale Forms can be purchased from a Treasury Cashier or from any Post Office.

Treasury Cashiers will sell dual numbered sets of Revenue Stamps and Second-Hand Sales Forms for a fee.

Note. Dual numbered means that there will be two stamps with the same number.

TC – 08

This is an illustration of Treasury Cashier Numbered Revenue Stamps.

For example, a person with PIT-C3-789/7890 buys a car from a seller SPIT-PRO1- 180/1236 for $23,370.00; the registration number is XX786XX

This is an illustration of the Numbered Revenue Stamp Receipt and how it should be recorded:

TAX CATEGORYPAY AS YOU EARN: PAYE - EMPLOYMENT

PAYE - CONTRACTS
PAYE - CIVIL SERVANTS
PAYE - BONUS

PAYE

EMPLOYERS AND THE MINISTRY OF LABOUR/DISTRICT LABOUR OFFICE

1. Any household or company which employs people must register with the District Employment Office (for statistics and tax purposes).
2. All employers must fill in a PAYE/Employment Form and receive their Permanent Employer Number.
3. Companies employing must attain a Display Certificate from the District Employment Office on a yearly basis as the employees will be entitled to a 'bonus' from their profits.
4. All taxes must be collected by the employer each month and forwarded to the District Employment PAYE Tax Office.
5. Trade unions will not be allowed in developing countries.
6. If the employee has complaints, they can go to the District Employment Officer, and if that fails to solve the issue [which is unlikely] they can then complain to the ombudsman. As a last resort, the employee can make use of Courts of Law.
7. The District Employment Office will keep statistics with regards to both employment and unemployment in the given district.
8. The C-18 Number will be the reference number for all employees.
9. PAYE/contract forms are obtainable from and registered at the District Employment Office. The person registering on PAYE will use their C-18 Number as a reference.
10. The employer must inform the District Employment Office if any employee is laid off.
11. Any person seeking employment must register with the District Employment Office and get a Permanent Number.
12. Employers wishing to employ skilled people should contact the District Employment Office.
13. The Treasury Cashier will collect all PAYE tax.
14. The Treasury Cashier will collect all PAYE contract tax.
15. The IncomeTax Department will operate with the District Employment Office and the Treasury Cashier.

PAYE

CIVIL SERVANTS/GOVERNMENT EMPLOYEES

To ensure an efficient and dedicated state/civil servant, and one who is unlikely to be tempted to engage in corrupt practices, a sufficient salary must be paid.

Low pay generally encourages corruption.

All civil servants should receive their wages/salaries through the bank. The monies will be available for withdrawal with an appropriate card at ATMs.

If any state/civil servant or politician is caught in corruption, they will be tried in court within 14 days.

1. They will be suspended from their post until the investigations are complete.
2. They will be required to fill Form C-18 in again, and this will be compared with their previous Form C-18, any excesses determining the allegations of corruption. (The filling in of Form C-18 will be for investigation purposes only.)
3. If the defendant cannot explain the surplus, the surplus will be confiscated.

If the state/civil servant is found guilty of corruption they will be dismissed from their job, fined or jailed.

There will be separate courts for civil servants and politicians in the capital.

The government will employ undercover agents to detect corrupt practices in state/civil servants. Entrapment or any other temptation will not be used, but observation and the gathering of evidence will be permitted.

Those who resist corruption will be rewarded and their position upgraded. This will be judged by their honest and dedicated performance of duty.

A corrupt politician or civil servant convicted of corruption will not be re-employed by the government or be able to enter any future contest for any parliamentary seat.

The government will reward the police force, undercover agent, or any civil servant who helps in recovering the losses from any robbery, drug gang activity, or from any other illegal activity.

The reward will be 10% of the recovered value of goods/property for the team.

To prevent road accidents and promote safety on the roads, the traffic police will be rewarded 10% of any fine.

All civil servants will be taxed as per the PAYE tax schedule.

PAYE/PAY AS YOU EARN – ALL EMPLOYMENT AND PAYE CONTRACTS

PAY TABLE

TAXES FOR ALL EMPLOYEMENT INCLUDING GOVERNMENT EMPLOYEES

LOW (L)

| From $20 to $67 | Tax to be deducted: 1% | Perks exempted |

MEDIUM LOW (ML)

| From $68 to $234 | Tax to be deducted: 4% | Perks exempted |

MEDIUM (M)

From $235 to $499	Tax to be deducted: 6%	Perks exempted
MEDIUM HIGH (MH)		
From $500 to $999	Tax to be deducted: 10%	Add perks
HIGH (H)		
From $1,000 up	Tax to be deducted: 20%	Add perks

Note: Please follow Regulation 7 for employers.

PAYE - 05

WORK CONTRACTS

A Work Contract can be defined as a fixed commitment for a certain project or assignment. Work Contracts apply mostly to entertainers, sportsman, journalists, musicians, etc.

The person entering the Work Contract will have to fill out a Work Contract Form and register it with the District Employment Office. There will be two forms. The first form, called the Work Contract, will have the full details of the employer and the details be filled in by the person entering into the contract, giving all the details of the terms and conditions and the value of the contract. The second form is the PAYE Tax Plan. Tax will be deducted by the contractor and submitted to the District Employment Office. The C-18 Number of the person will be recorded.

So, for example – a certain actor has a work contract with a filmmaker for $9,000 for a particular film. The terms and conditions are that the actor will be paid $300 per day, which will be deducted from the agreed sum of $9,000.

The first week, the actor works for a day and receives $300. The second week, he works for three days and receives $900. In the third week, he works for five days and receives $1,500. There is no work in the fourth week of the month.

This is how his pay will be deducted.

First week pay = $300 @ Rate – (M) Medium @ 6%	= $ 18.00
Second week pay = $900 @ Rate – (MH) M High @ 10%	= $ 90.00
Third week pay = $1,500 @ Rate – (H) High @ 20%	= $300

This is an example of how the tax is deducted; it will be collected by the employer who will fill in monthly PAYE/Tax Returns and send the monies collected to the Income Tax Department or the Treasury Cashier.

Note: If the earnings of the film actor exceed $10,000, he will have to follow Regulation 6 and submit annual accounts.

The actor has paid $408 in tax on his earnings; this will not need to be paid again when he submits his accounts.

BONUS

Every employee should be entitled to a bonus at the end of the year if they have been in employment continuously for the full year. The company or the employer will distribute 25% of their net profit (tax paid) to all employees.

If it is private company or employer, they may include the domestic employees in the list.

In many countries, particularly in Africa and Asia, the employer will see high profits – and they'll be able to buy property, expensive cars and watch their bank balances grow, while their employees struggle to make ends meet. It is only fair that some of these profits should be shared, and extended to employees, as these profits originate – in good part – from their sweat and toil.

This is also to reduce the gap between rich and poor.

So, a bonus will be paid and the employees will not be required to pay any tax on it because it will be tax paid by the employer. The bonus will be by a cheque issued by the employer, for the purposes of accountability.

RANKS IN BONUS:

CEO/MANAGER   X 5
ALL OTHERS   X 3

Supposing Company XY has 23 employees and 1 CEO and the Tax Paid Net Profit is $450,000; this is how the net profit will be shared:

25% of $450,000 is $112,500

$112,500 is then to be shared.

The company has 23 employees x 3 = 69, one CEO/manager x 5 = 74.

So, the $112,500 needs to be divided into 74 shares. One share = $1,520.27

CEO/MANAGER x 5 $1520.27 = $7601.35

ALL OTHERS x 3 $1520.27 = $4560.81

Twenty-five per cent is a fair percentage when it comes to sharing the net profit of companies, both large and small.

Sharing net profits in this way will promote loyalty and dedication amongst employees and eliminate strikes.

Please refer Regulation 11 on Page 160.

TREASURY CASHIERS AND DISTRICT TAX OFFICES

THE FUNCTIONS OF THE TREASURY CASHIER

Q1. WHAT IS A TREASURY CASHIER'S ROLE?

Treasury Cashier are the government's agents/agencies office that pays and receives monies.

The District Tax Office can also be used for this purpose.

All Treasury Cashiers will have identification numbers.

Taxpayers, according to their Tax Categories, will be referred to the Treasury Cashier by the Income Tax Department.

Those in the PIT-C Tax Category (large companies) may deal directly with the Income Tax Department, bypassing Treasury Cashiers.

DSSs with remittance cheques can be posted.

Treasury Cashiers will open a file on each taxpayer within their Tax Category.

Licence Numbers will be used for identification on each file, along with a Treasury Cashier Allocation Number.

Treasury Cashiers will be authorised by the Income Tax Department to register and give file numbers to (all) tax categories, based on their Licence Number.

For example:

XYZ Enterprises are wholesalers and registered with Treasury Cashier No. 70 under the Licence No. PIT-C3/234/7890

This being so, the Treasury Cashier will open a file for them; the number on the file will be PIT-C3/234/7890 BLT2 [note- 7890 is the C-18 Number].

PIT-C3	=	Tax Category (Wholesaler)
234.	=	IncomeTax Sequence Number of the Tax Category
7890BLT2	=	C-18 Number

Only cheques will be allowed for DSS and PAYE remittances.

The Treasury Cashier will record and send all of the following transactions to the Income Tax Department.

TREASURY CASHIERS

THE SELLING AND RECORDING OF VARIOUS RECEIPTS/FORMS

1. PIT-C Receipts.
2. SPIT- Receipts.

3. TicketTax Books.
4. Daily Sales Sheets (DSSs).
5. Numbered Revenue Stamps.
6. Second-Hand Item Forms.
7. Daily Sales Sheets, PIT-C8 (gambling).
8. Daily Sales Sheets, SPIT-GMB1 (gambling).
9. PAYE Contract Forms
10. Employee's Tax Collection Forms

RECORDING THE TRANSACTIONS

All Tax Categories referred by the Income Tax Department will have an individual file for the collection of Provisional Tax.

Treasury Cashiers will enter the following transactions:

- Selling of PIT-C and SPIT- Receipts (if bought from the TC).
- Selling of TicketTax Books (if bought from the TC).
- Selling of DSSs to the PIT-C/SPIT-/gambling.
- Selling the forms for second-hand items and Numbered Revenue Stamps.
- Issuing Consent Receipts for Sales Vouchers/PIT-C /SPIT-/TicketTax Tickets (if self-printed).
- Issuing Acknowledgment Receipts for DSSs and Provisional Income Tax received for the month.
- Banking all monies received.

As there will be many transactions; all monies received must be properly recorded and entered into the accounts.

When depositing money, each section must have a code for quick auditing.

001 / PIT-C Receipts.
002 / SPIT- Receipts.
003 / Ticket Books.
004 / Daily Sales Sheets.
005 / Numbered Revenue Stamps.
006 / Second-hand items.
007 / Daily Sales Sheet/PIT-C8/gambling.
008 / Employee's Tax Collection Forms

TREASURY CASHIER PROCESSES AND PROCEDURES

TICKETTAX:

Tax prepaid ticket books can be purchased from Treasury Cashiers.

A Consent Receipt will indicate the numbers registered and tax paid.

Companies can print their own tickets. Consent receipts may be obtained prior to the printing of tickets, so that consent numbers can be included in the printing.

The Consent Receipt will be given on each ticket's book value.

So, supposing a bus company wants ten books printed, with $1, $2, $3, $5, $10, and $20 tickets. A Consent Receipt will be issued separately for each ticket book's value, starting from $1, starting to end numbers of the vouchers.

NUMBERED REVENUE STAMPS: SET OF TWO STAMPS OF THE SAME NUMBER

Numbered Revenue Stamps and forms for sale of second-hand items from $250 will only be available from Treasury Cashiers.

Treasury Cashiers will issue receipts for NRS [Numbered Revenue Stamps] and will write in the receipt the name of the item and its serial number, to the person sold and value with their Tax or C-18 Number. The seller will be taxed @ 10% and retain the receipt. The NRS will be affixed on both the seller's as well the buyer's form.

REGIONAL INCOME TAX DEPARTMENT

All Treasury Cashiers under the jurisdiction of the Regional Income Tax Department (RITD) will send the Provisional Tax collected with the relevant documents to the RITD.

The RITD will send all DSSs to their respective District Offices within the complex.

The RITD office will record the transactions from each line of the DSS in the tax payer categories individual file.

In this way, the accounting will be completed, even for non-licenced and non-accounting earners.

TREASURY CASHIER CONSENT RECEIPTS

What is a Treasury Cashier Consent Receipt?

A Treasury Cashier Consent Receipt is a receipt issued by a Treasury Cashier upon registration of the numbers from beginning to end for all types of voucher books – cash sales books, invoice books, debit note books, credit note books, PIT-C and SPIT- Receipts and ticket books.

The Treasury Cashier will register the beginning and end number of each voucher book.

Sales Vouchers or self-printed PIT-C/SPIT- tickets will not be valid without Consent Numbers.

Sales Vouchers, receipts or tickets without Consent Receipt Numbers will be subject to tax-avoidance penalties.

The receipt is also called a 'TCCR', short for 'Treasury Cashier Consent Receipt.

The 'TCCR' needs to be quoted on DSS returns and also on PIT-C/SPIT-/Sales Vouchers/tickets.

If PIT-C Receipt Books and SPIT- Receipts are purchased from Treasury Cashiers, the TCCR needs to be quoted on all pages of the receipt books.

If PIT-C/SPIT-/cash sales/invoices/debit notes/credit notes are printed by the Tax Category holder, they can be registered in bulk according to category, and a TCCR obtained separately for each.

Treasury Cashiers will charge a small fee for registration, at 50c per 100-page book.

The TCCR Number must be written on the cover of each book, for ease of inspection.

Treasury Cashiers will have separate cards on file, as per licence and Tax Category.

For example:

A PIT-C3 wholesaler wants to register 10 Cash Sale Books, Numbers 1000 to 2000, and five Invoices Books Numbers 500 to 1000.

This is how they will be registered:

(1) TC70/PIT-C3/234/4567BLT1 – C/S 1000–2000 (10) (on the cash sale card).
(2) TC70/PIT-C3/234/4567BLT1 – INV 500–1000 (5) (on the invoice card).

The date, numbers and 'TCCR' must be entered in record cards.

This will be registered on two 'TCCR' Receipts, as there are two varieties of books being registered.

All Tax Categories need to keep duplicates of the used books for five years.

Refer for a Consent Receipt Illustration.

TREASURY CASHIER PROCESSES AND PROCEDURES

DAILY SALES SHEETS: DSS

Daily Sales Sheets are compulsory for all PIT-C and SPIT- categories/gambling.

The front part of the DSS will record the licence, PIT-C or SPIT- Receipt Number, Voucher Number and the amount of tax collected.

The back will have recorded credit notes and unpaid returned cheques.

An illustration of a Daily Sales Sheet is on page

ACKNOWLEDGEMENT RECEIPT

An Acknowledgement Receipt will be issued by the Treasury Cashier once they receive all DSSs, as well as the Provisional Tax collected for the month, from the registered taxpayer.

When the Acknowledgement Receipt is issued, the taxpayer will not be queried for the month in question by the Regional Income Tax Department.

See the illustration on page

(**Tax avoidance detection**) The introduction of various vouchers, receipts and the DSS for the selling of goods will tighten accountability. Any corrupt activity will be subject to obstacles and become harder to complete. So, if a shop is stocked to the hilt, but without enough Purchase Vouchers to justify the stocks, an enquiry will be launched. The enquiry will be undertaken by the Regional Income Tax Department, which will have the appropriate file. All purchases will have been recorded in the DSS in the file, enabling comparison. Any excess of stock will then be determined, and the Regional Income Tax Departmentwill then need to ascertain whether there has been tax avoidance. If there is an imbalance, there will be enough evidence to convict the suspect.

TREASURY CASHIER PROCESSES AND PROCEDURES

PAYE:

All PAYE employees will have to be registered at the District Employment Office and get their Permanent Identification Number.

THE TREASURY CASHIER'S ROLE:

The Treasury Cashierwill receive payroll sheets from all employers, every month.

The payroll will contain breakdowns of the wages/salaries of all employees.

INCOME TAX OFFICE:

The Treasury Cashierwill put all payrolls in order, and calculate a grand total for the month.

The Treasury Cashierwill send all monies received from employers (payroll) to the Income Tax Department.

BANK:

All the monies received will be banked, using a sort code for PAYE.

STATISTICS OFFICE:

The total figures of employees, and the amount of tax collected for the month, will be forwarded to the Statistics Office by the Regional Income Tax Department.

Note: The statistics of the persons in employment and the persons not in employment will be available.

TREASURY CASHIER PROCESSES AND PROCEDURES

PAYE/CONTRACTS:

Treasury Cashiers will sell triplicate PAYE/contract forms.

There will be an office in the Ministry of Employment (District Office) to receive and transact PAYE/contract agreements.

The employer or contractor will be liable to collecting tax as per the PAYE table (see page

The employer will record all the tax collected on the payroll.

The payroll will then be submitted, either to the Treasury Cashieror the Regional Income Tax Department, at the end of the month.

INCOME TAX DEPARTMENT:

All monies collected from the accumulated payrolls will be forwarded to the Income Tax Department.

BANK:

All monies will be banked, using the appropriate sort code for PAYE/contracts.

STATISTICS:

The Treasury Cashieror the Employment Office will send the figures of PAYE/contract monies collected in the month to the Statistics Department.

PAYE/contract will be filed at the Ministry of Labour/Employment.

PENDING LEGISLATION REGULATIONS: 1 TO 42

TO PUT INTO LEGISLATION:

1. P150 – Mandatory Legislation A to G – Licence
2. P151 – Registering business names

3. P152 – Tax Number – Vote Roll Number
4. P153 – Treasury Cashier (use)
5. P154 – Current bank account
6. P155 – Bookkeeping/accounting
7. P156 – Employer's/PAYE contracts
8. P157 – Governmental procurement of goods and services
9. P158 – Privatised government parastatals or NGO franchise holdings
10. P159 – No Licence Holder or NLH under $10,000 capital
11. P160 – Employees and Employers
12. P161 – Industry
13. P162 – Accidental loss or act of God
14. P163 – Late submission of accounts
15. P164 – Associations
16. P165 – Tax Clearance Certificate
17. P166 – Will/inheritance/probate/executors
18. P167 – Bankruptcy
19. P168 – Amnesty
20. P169 – 20% tax theory
21. P170 – Gifts
22. P171 – Company and private company
23. P172 – Tax evading penalties
24. P173 – Compensations
25. P174 – Retailers
26. P175 – Trade mark brands
27. P176 – Exports
28. P177 – Contractors
29. P178 – Partners
30. P179 – Court cases
31. P180 – Religious and charity imports
32. P181 – Control on expenses
33. P182 – Foreign aid or loans
34. P183 – Price controlled items
35. P184 – Depreciation/appreciation
36. P185 – Stock Inventories
37. P186 – Imports
38. P187 – Capital Gains Tax
39. P188 – Renewal of C-18 Forms every five years
40. P189 – Civil servants
41. P190 – Free medical care for exempts and employees in PAYE category up to [M]
42. P191 – Exempt categories 1-5

MANDATORY [PENDING LEGISLATION]

A. Form C-18
B. Vote Roll or Tax Number.
C. Tax Category.

D. National Housing and Social Welfare Fund.
E. Stocks inventories with annual tax returns.
F. Voting at the constituency.
G. 25% tax paid profits to be shared by all employees.

PENDING LEGISLATION REGULATION 1: LICENCE

1. Capital from $10,000 and up: all taxpayers will require a licence for their businesses, professions or occupations.
2. Registration of business or personal name: To obtain a licence, the taxpayer will have to register their name or business name with the Registrar of Business Names.
3. Tax Card Number with C-18 Number: This card number will be required when applying for a licence.
4. Current bank account number: This number will be required when applying for the licence.
5. Appointing a bookkeeper/auditor: A bookkeeping firm or auditor will be required when applying for the licence.
6. Ministry: The licence will be issued by the appropriate ministry; for example, if a licence required is for retail, the Ministry of Trade and Industry will issue the licence.
7. Permanent Licence Number: The ministry will grant the applicant a licence with a permanent number in their Tax Category. For example, if the applicant is a retailer with the registered trade name of NBD Retailers in Tax Category PIT-P2, the ministry will give them their permanent number in sequence order of application, which is 2234 followed by the C-18 Number. The Permanent Licence Number of NBD Retailers will thus be PIT-P2/2234/12388BLT2. For all business endeavours, this Permanent Licence Number will have to be used. If the business closes, the number will be struck off from the sequence order [not the C-18 Number] and will not be given to any other taxpayer in that category.
8. Renewal: The licence needs to be renewed every year, and fees will apply.
9. The licence is revocable: The licence can be revoked by court order after the licence holder pays 11 tax penalties or more. This will be enforced for five years.
10. If the taxpayer on 1-9 requires a licence again, they may apply after 36 months. The taxpayer will need to give new details on 1-2 and 1-4.

Note: If the licence is granted after 36 months, it will be given a new Permanent Licence Number and the licensee will have to use another business name.

PENDING LEGISLATION REGULATION 2: REGISTERING OF BUSINESS NAMES, PARTNERSHIPS AND COMPANIES, AND LIMITED AND PRIVATE LIMITED COMPANIES

(1) THE REQUIREMENT TO REGISTER PERSONAL OR COMPANY NAMES

Form C-18: Tax Clearance Certificate to know the capital.
A C-18 Vote/Tax Card Number will be required.
In the case of a partnership or company, all the partners' C-18 Vote/Tax Card Numbers will be required.

(2) PARTNERSHIPS AND COMPANIES

All partners need to fill in a special form for the partnership or company. The total amount of capital of the company must be stated. Each individual's share, in terms of amount and percentage, must be stated.

(3) The name, company can only be used if it is in partnership, limited or private limited company.

(4) The limited company will be for the partners, all (or part) of their total capital as on the current Tax Clearance Certificate will be the figures of their limited company.

For example, if the total amount the three partners would like to invest in the company is $3m, then $3m will be their limit (liability). The suppliers (creditors/banks) have the right to inspect the balance sheet to determine the debt of the company, if the creditors/banks risk borrowing more than the company's liability, they will incur the loss (in case of bankruptcy).

(5) Private limited companies can be registered by individuals or by family members who are in business together. Their recent Tax Clearance Certificates will be the figures of their private limited, liability [capital].

PENDING LEGISLATION REGULATION 3: MANDATORY TAX NUMBER

1. The Tax Number: The Tax Number is mandatory and will be given by the Regional IncomeTax Headquarters according to the person's Tax Category in sequence order of their registration followed by the C-18 Number.
2. Partnership: A person can be a partner in many companies. The Tax Number will be different and will be according to the Tax Category of their trade or occupation, but the C-18 Number of a person will remain the same.
3. Companies and partners: Companies will pay tax using their licence and Tax Category Number.
4. The profits in the company will be divided according to their shares and will be put in their personal bank accounts. The tax will be paid by the company.
5. Exemption: If the person in an exempt category reaches the $10,000 capital mark, they will be given a Tax Number in their Tax Category and will be registered with the Regional IncomeTax Office who will categorise them into their respective Tax Category and give them a Permanent Tax Number.
6. This is how the Tax Number will be allocated: For example, a wholesaler – Tab Wholesalers in Tax Category PIT-C3 whose C-18 Number is 12345BLT4 is being registered at the Regional IncomeTax Headquarters. This is how the tax official will give the Tax Number. The tax official will see the previous registered number in the wholesaler category and the last number registered was 3456, so the official will give this wholesaler the Number 3457. Therefore, the Tab Wholesalers number will be PIT-C3/3457/12345BLT4. This will be the Permanent Number for Tab Wholesalers. PIT-C3/3457 is the wholesale Tax Category Number and /12345BLT4 is the C-18 Vote Roll Number; BLT means Blantmont District and 4 means the Blantmont constituency number.

PENDING LEGISLATION REGULATION 4: TREASURY CASHIERS/THE DISTRICT TAX OFFICE

1. The deadline to submit the DSS and Provisional Tax will be the 10th of the following month. So, for example, all of the transactions for January must be submitted by the 10th February.
2. Late submission of DSSs and Provisional Tax: The taxpayer will be liable to a penalty if they don't send their DSS by the deadline. The penalty will be 1% of the total tax collected, per each delayed day. The maximum waiting period will be up until the end of the month. So, for example, January's DSSs will be waited upon until the end of February and thereafter an investigation will be launched.
3. All payments above $500 must be made by cheque.
4. Consent Receipts: All Sales Vouchers, PIT-C and SPIT- Receipts and TicketTaxes require a Consent Receipt.
5. Acknowledgement Receipts: Acknowledgement Receipts will be issued upon receiving the month's DSS and Provisional Tax.
6. All tax collected will be banked into the Regional IncomeTax Department's account.

PENDING LEGISLATION REGULATION 5: CURRENT BANK ACCOUNT

1. Requirement: All Tax Categories are required to have a current bank account.
2. C-18 Vote/Tax Card Number: This will be required when opening a current bank account.
3. Registration of the business name: This certificate is required to open a current bank account. The bank account will be opened in the name appearing on the business name.
4. Licence: A photocopy of the licence must be given to the bank.
5. Import quotas: Import quotas will be through one bank account.
6. Payment by cheque to Treasury Cashiers: Treasury Cashiers will accept cheques only for payments above $500.
7. A Tax Clearance Certificate photocopy will be required by the bank. This is to record the capital of the person or company so that no excessive monies are deposited into the account.

PENDING LEGISLATION REGULATION 6: BOOKKEEPING/ACCOUNTING

1. Capital amount at $10,000 plus: Taxpayers with $10,000 in capital and above are required to undertake bookkeeping.
2. Sales turnovers from $100,000: If the sales turnover of the trader or service provider is over $100,000, then bookkeeping is required.
3. End of financial year is to be 31st December: The accounting financial year will fall on 31st December, to keep track of the year; this will enable people to keep track of one year, rather than combining two.
4. Appointing a bookkeeper: The taxpayer must appoint a bookkeeper. Having a bookkeeper is required to obtain a licence.
5. Deadline for the submitting of accounts: Five months will be allowed for the submitting of a tax assessment. So, for example, as the tax year ends on 31st December, the latest date to submit accounts will be the 31st May.
6. Penalty: If the accounts are submitted for tax assessment after 31st May; the tax assessments will be based straight on the gross profit or no business expenses can be claimed.

7. Exempted accounts [capital under $10,000] tax records will be undertaken by the Regional Income Tax Department. All the purchases or the services tax received by Tax Categories will be recorded in the DSS. Using the DSS, income tax officials will record each instance of purchases or obtained services in the file of every Tax Category Number. The tax will be totalled to see if it reaches the $10,000 ceiling.

8. Tax paid shares will be recorded in each individual's capital account, using their C-18 Vote/ Tax Card Number. So, for example, Mr X and his C-18 Vote/Card Number have shares in two companies. With the first company, SS Manufacturing Ltd, the tax paid share received was $40,000, and with the second company, TTT Transport, the tax paid share received was $30,000. The accountant, when doing his personal accounts based on the C-18 Vote/Tax Number, will add onto in the capital account the shares from SS Manufacturing ($40,000) and TTT Transport ($30,000).

PENDING LEGISLATION REGULATION 7: EMPLOYER/PAYE CONTRACTS

1. Registering of employees. All employees must be registered with the Employment Office by the employer.
2. Commercial employees. Commercial employees will pay tax as per the tax table on Page. The tax collected will be entered onto the payroll.
3. Domestic employees. All domestic employees will pay tax as per the tax table on Page. The tax collected by the employer will be entered onto the payroll.
4. Display Certificate of Employees. All commercial employers will be required to display a Certificate of Employees. This certificate will be filled by the employer who will give a photocopy to the District Employment Office who will then stamp the original certificate to endorse the certificate and acknowledge registration. An illustration of the certificate can be found on Page
5. All employees must register with the District Employment Office to get a Permanent Employment Number.
6. Deadline for submitting payroll/PAYE contract payments. The deadline will fall on the10th of the next month. So, for example, for payroll/PAYE collected for January, the deadline for remittance will fall on 10th February.
7. Disputes. All disputes will be handled by the Ministry of Employment. Trade unions will not be allowed in developing countries.
8. PAYE contracts and agreements. All PAYE contracts and agreements must be registered with the Ministry of Employment.
9. Any person or company who contracts will be liable for tax collections.
10. Civil servants. Salaries will be paid directly into bank accounts. Monies can be withdrawn by an ATM card.
11. All employees [combined] will be entitled to 25% [bonus] of tax paid profits of their employer.

PENDING LEGISLATION REGULATION 8: GOVERNMENTAL PROCUREMENT OF GOODS AND SERVICES

The Ministry of Finance will reserve all procurement monies in the annual budget to be used when and where necessary by all ministries and parastatals. A new Central Procurement Office [CPO]will be opened. The procedures will be like this:

a) Proposals. Example – the Ministry of Energy wants to procure 1,000 treated poles for their parastatal, the Electricity Company.
b) The CPO will enter into their list.
c) The CPO will engage private surveyors to scrutinise the requirements.
d) The CPO will then place the request in sequence order of urgency or national priority.
e) Tenders will be advertised.
f) The CPO will invite officials from the ministry concerned and also Ministry of Finance officials to award the contract.

1. A licence will be required to supply goods, services or contracts to government ministries. The licence fee will be $1,000 per annum. The licence will clearly specify the designated group supplier.
2. Description of items to supply. This needs to be clearly stated with a brand name/trade mark and the price list submitted every six months.
3. Designated group. The supplier must be from a designated group or specialising in particular items.
4. Profit control. All supplies, services, contracts to the government are entitled to 20% profit on cost.
5. No tenders. No advertisement will be placed by the ministries for the supplying of goods. Letters will be sent to the designated supplier's group for the items required.
6. Sharing the supply of the common item/commodity/services. The supplies will be shared by the suppliers of the common items. (See example, below.)
7. Tax Category SPIT/GMS1, for suppliers to the government. This Tax Category is for all suppliers and service providers @ 4% SPIT.
8. Tax Clearance Certificate capital figure. The supplier's Tax Clearance Certificate capital figure will be examined before the licence is issued, to ascertain if the Tax Category supplier is capable of supplying goods or services.
9. Building/road contracts. This will require tenders. They will have to adhere to the government procurement regulations.
10. Big projects require tenders.
11. The government will pay in stages after the completion of the (scheduled) inspected work.

PENDING LEGISLATION REGULATION 9: PRIVATISED GOVERNMENT PARASTATALS OR NGO – FRANCHISE HOLDINGS

The government parastatals are:

1. Water supply.
2. Electricity supply.
3. Ground line telephones.
4. Airlines.
5. Forestry.
6. Radio stations.
7. TV stations.
8. Railways.

9. Mines.
10. Mobile phones.

If the government allows the privatisation of any of its parastatals, then they will become NGO's franchise holdings.

1. All franchise holdings will be placed in the Self Provisional Tax Category SPIT/PST 1-10.
2. The SPIT/FRN 1-10 tax rate will be 10%.
3. SPIT/PST and SPIT/FRN will be valid as business expenses in the account books.

PENDING LEGISLATION REGULATION 10:

NON-LICENCE HOLDER OR NLH

1. Non-licenced retailers/hawkers will not be required to do bookkeeping or keep accounts.
2. If the sales turnover is less than $100,000.00 per annum, then accounting will not be required.
3. If the capital is less than $10,000.00 per annum, then the person need not do any accounts.
4. The Regional Income Tax Headquarters will give them a Tax Category Number according to their business or if they are providing services according to their occupation
5. The NLH will not be required to have a licence, to register their business or to open up a bank account

PENDING LEGISLATION REGULATION 11: EMPLOYEES & EMPLOYERS

BONUS:

- Every employee [commercial or domestic] is entitled to 25% shared profits of their employer [tax paid].
- Because the bonus is tax paid by the employer, the employee will not pay any tax on it.
- Ranks in bonus: The CEO/Manager will get x5 and all the other employees will get x3.
- Example – A company has one CEO/Manager and 23 employees and the tax paid profit of the company is $450,000.
- Share workout: 25% [workers' share] of $450,000 is $112,500. Therefore 1 CEO x 5 = 5 + 23 employees x3 = 69 + 5 ≈74. Therefore, divide $112,500 by 74 = $1,520.27 per share. So, the CEO gets $1,520.27 x 5 = $7,601.35. The other employees get $1,520.27 x3 = $4,560.81

MEDICAL AID – WITH GOVERNMENT HOSPITALS

- All employers will have to get Medical Aid for their employees to be treated at the government hospitals or clinics.

NO TRADE OR LABOUR UNIONS WILL BE ALLOWED

- Trade or labour unions damage, intimidate and disturb the system and therefore are not required.
- All labour disputes will be handled by the Ministry of Labour or, if it fails, then by the ombudsman, or if that fails thrn by the magistrate courts. The process must have results within a maximum of six months.

Note – All other labour laws of the land will apply.

PENDING LEGISLATION REGULATION 12: INDUSTRY

1. Customs Tariff: There will be only one Customs Duty Tariff.
2. Industries will pay 20% less custom duties on imports.
3. Bonded warehouses, for the storage of raw materials, will not be allowed for industries.
4. Half of custom duties can be paid by instalments. To compensate for the restrictions on bonded warehouse(s), the government will accept half of the custom duty payments on raw materials; the remaining half can be paid by instalments over 12 months.
5. There will be no dutyfree concessions on industrial items, as this leads to corruption.

PENDING LEGISLATION REGULATION 13: ACCIDENTAL LOSS/LOSS THROUGH ACT OF GOD/ROBBERY/INVESTMENTS/FIRE:

1. Accidental loss without insurance. If the taxpayer happens to incur an accidental loss and has no insurance, they can fill in Form RUG 13 at the Police Station. (This is an Income Tax Police Statement.)
2. Accidental loss, partly paid by insurance. All assets will be noted in the account books; the partial loss may be deducted from the insurance pay-out, and the remaining loss recorded in Form RUG 13.
3. Loss through an act of God. If the loss is through an act of God, all losses should be detailed and attached to Form RUG 13.
4. Robbery. If a business is robbed, an inventory should be made of the stock and the full loss determined. If it is cash that is stolen, the amount can be worked out by using the Daily Sales Sheets and the last bank deposit. The amount stolen should then be reported in Form RUG 13.
5. RUG 13. This is a police statement form for Income Tax purposes, which will be dated. If any recovery is made, it will be deducted from the first RUG 13 and carry forward onto a new RUG 13. The first RUG 13 will remain in the file.
6. Investments. Investments are shares and stocks, investments in bricks and mortar, land and buildings. If there is any loss on this, written proof from the brokers or real estate agents and a valuation report will be required.
7. Fire. With regarded to loss by fire, remaining assets should be accounted for, then the previous year's balance sheet obtained and the amount deducted. This balance should then be recorded on Form RUG 13.
8. Fraud. The penalty will be ten times the value of the amount claimed. Police officers, if proven guilty in a court case, will also pay ten times the value of fraud, or in lieu face a jail sentence.
9. Income Tax Department. The Income Tax Department will accept the losses as detailed on Form RUG 13 and this will be reduced on the capital account for accountability.

PENDING LEGISLATION REGULATION 14: LATE SUBMISSION OF ACCOUNTS

1. Submission of accounts deadline. The accounts must be submitted by the deadline date, 31st December.

2. Five months grace period. Five months grace period will be extended for the submitting of accounts, up to 31st May.
3. Submission of accounts after 31st May. When this is the case, the account will be assessed on the basis of gross profits. This is the penalty, with late submission; no business expenses can be deducted.

PENDING LEGISLATION REGULATION 15: ASSOCIATION

1. Compulsory membership – for professionals, suppliers to governmental ministries, investors, landlords, all road cargo and passenger vehicles, entertainment groups and all sporting clubs.
2. Grievances from association members – will be heard and responded to by the appropriate ministry.
3. New regulations from the government – may be discussed in the monthly or quarterly meetings.
4. Recommendations – will be taken from the association to rectify some by-laws.

PENDING LEGISLATION REGULATION 16: TAX CLEARANCE CERTIFICATE

1. The Tax Clearance Certificate acts as proof that tax has been paid for the financial year and is up to date and will be required to register the business name.
2. TCCs will be issued when the taxpayer leaves the country, to prove that all taxes have been paid.
3. TCCs will be issued after the completion of the probate process, to prove that inheritors have paid the deceased's taxes.
4. TCCs will be issued to people under fraud investigation, who have been cleared or have paid all charges.
5. TCCs will be issued to taxpayers who have made a gift of an asset where the tax has been paid.
6. TCCs will be issued to Amnesty Groups B and C to prove that they are in clear of **all** tax arrears.
7. Purchase limit – the TCC holder will be able to spend 20% of their value in capital (10) for any one purchase. If the amount is in excess of the 20% limit, then the TCC will be required.

CODE FOR CAPITAL TO BE WRITTEN IN THE TCC – (10)
$10,000 = 10K $111,000 = 111K $999,000 = 999K
$1,550,000 = 1.550M $987,670,000 = 987.67M

8. If the exempt Tax Category citizen purchases any good that is over $500, this must have a TCC.

PENDING LEGISLATION REGULATION 17: WILLS/ INHERITANCE/PROBATE/ EXECUTORS

1. Wills. It will be compulsory for people with capital exceeding $10,000 to make a will and appoint a lawyer.

2. Registering and depositing of the will. The will needs to be registered and deposited with the Registrar of Birth, Deaths & Wills. The registrar will supply a reference number.

3. Requirements of wills. Two witnesses outside the family need to sign the will.

4. Trustee. Any person making a will whose children are under age should appoint two trustees. These two trustees will sign as witnesses to the will.

5. Death Certificate. A Death Certificate will be required before burial. It can be obtained from the District Commissioner, the Constituency Office, or from the Registrar of Birth, Deaths & Wills.

6. Lawyers. Only the appointed lawyer will be able to obtain the will from the Registrar of Births, Deaths & Wills. The lawyer will read the will in front of family members, and if there are no minors in the will, the lawyer will start proceedings for probate. If the will has appointed two trustees, the lawyer will obtain probate and hand it over to the trustees.

7. Probate procedures are to be completed within 12 months. Probate must be completed within 12 months. If the probate is not completed within 12 months, then the court will rule and give directions.

8. Inheritor(s) can continue the trade/services or any other occupation of the deceased, until probate is executed.

9. A will can be changed as many times as the person wants; when this happens, the old will must be destroyed by the Registrar of Births, Deaths & Will.

10. An exempt Tax Category person with no will: People in the exempt Tax Category who have no will will be dealt with by the Constituency Office. The person will be issued with a Death Certificate and all that is left behind by the deceased will be shared to all people who live in his/her house and nothing to outsiders. The Resident MP will act as executor.

PENDING LEGISLATION REGULATION 18: VOLUNTARY CLOSURE OF BUSINESS/BANKRUPTCY

VOLUNTARY CLOSURE OF BUSINESS OR SERVICE:

1. Form RUG18 can only be completed after all creditors have been paid and there is no remaining debt.

2. A Tax Clearance Certificate Number needs to be written on Form RUG18.

BANKRUPTCY/INSOLVANCY:

1. The reason for bankruptcy must be established from the auditing of accounts. The following factors could contribute to bankruptcy:
   a) Losses in shares/stocks.
   b) Losses from robbery – Form 13.
   c) Excessive bad debts – Court case numbers will be required.
   d) Losses due to court cases/fines/penalties.
   e) Natural disasters/acts of God – Form 13.
   f) Accidental losses – Form 13.
   g) Failing sales and high overheads.
   h) Other genuine reasons.

This must be looked into by the IncomeTax investigating team.

(1) The bankruptcy cannot be registered if assets reach 70% of the value of the debt – the court must rule to give more time to pay debts.
(2) Form RUG18 will be issued by the court to confirm the bankruptcy.
(3) The creditors will divide whatever is left after administration expenses.
(4) Independent agents will be appointed by the government to dispose of stocks, assets, etc.
(5) If the bankruptcy is fraudulent, the perpetrator will be penalised; this will be in the form of a prison sentence, or if found with any remaining assets passed on to a third party.
(6) Those who have been bankrupted will be debarred from obtaining another licence for five years. Those who are involved in fraud will not be able to work in that Tax Category.
(7) The bankrupted may be investigated at any time if they are caught spending more than the Tax Clearance Certificate.

PENDING LEGISLATION REGULATION 19: AMNESTY

GROUP A: ASSETS ALREADY DECLARED

Group A is for those citizens who have already declared their assets and have paid tax on it.

- Their properties will be valued as per the current market value and they will have to pay Capital Gains Tax

GROUP B: DECLARING ASSETS IN THE AMNESTY PERIOD

Group B will be for those citizens who declare hidden assets or assets that have not been recorded in the account books.
The amnesty will be that no questions will be asked if:

1. The undeclared property is over 10 years old and had not been declared to evade tax.
2. If the property is built, bought or transferred into the name of a family member who is not paying taxes or who cannot justify its ownership must be transferred back to the proper owner who bought it, otherwise it will be confiscated.

The Capital Gains Tax will not be backdated but it will have to be paid in the amnesty period.

*After the assets are classified as clean, the Tax Clearance Certificate will be issued.

GROUP C: NOT DECLARING ASSETS IN THE AMNESTY PERIOD

Group C is composed of those citizens who fail to declare their assets within the amnesty period.
If at any time they are caught, they will have to explain and if the explanation is unsatisfactory and not justifiable with IncomeTax declarations than the asset(s) will be confiscated.
If the matter is of negligence then the person will have to pay a penalty and will have to pay tax; this will be after a thorough investigations.
An investigation will commence immediately to determine if the assets are from (i) corruption, (ii) drugs, (iii) robbery, or (iv) tax avoidance.
Any such assets will be forfeited by Court Order and the person will have to answer charges.

PENDING LEGISLATION REGULATION 20: 20% TAX THEORY

All businesses and services have a certain level of average profit margins, worked out in percentages.

A wholesaler's assumed average profit margin could be 15%, whilst a retailer's assumed average profit margin could be around 20%.

In this system, all 20 tax categories will have their tax rates based on the assumed average profit margin worked out in percentages.

The tax calculations used will be based on the central figure of 20 per cent (20%).

This is how a wholesaler's 15% assumed profit will be worked out to their tax rate. To find out the 20% tax rate on the 15% profit margin; 20 being the 5th part of 100, 5 will be the dividing figure; 15 divided by 5 = 3. The tax rate of the wholesaler will thus be 3%.

For example, the wholesaler purchases from an industrial company goods worth $15,000. The industrial company will charge the wholesaler 3% on the PIT-C2 Receipt, which will amount to $450. The industrial company has collected a Provisional Tax of $450 on behalf of the wholesaler and will forward it to the Income Tax Department through the District Tax Office.

The wholesaler has paid a Provisional Income Tax of $450 on their profits, and this will be accumulated for 12 months, up to the end of the financial year. The audited accounts will be assessed and all the Provisional Tax paid will be deducted from the Annual Tax Assessments.

PENDING LEGISLATION REGULATION 21: GIFTS

1. Taxpayers in any category can give a gift to any person using their C-18 Number.
2. The person who presents the gift must have a Tax Clearance Certificate.
3. If the gift is taxable, then the recipient will be liable to taxes on it (in the future) and will have to register the gift in the relevant Tax Category.
4. There will be a special Tax Clearance Certificate for gifts, which will include the following important information:
   a) The name and C-18 Vote/Tax Card Number of the person who presented the gift.
   b) The date the gift was given.
   c) A description of the gift and serial/deed numbers.
   d) The date of the gift bought by the presenter.
   e) The actual value of the gift.
   f) Proof of the tax paid for it.
   g) The reason for the gift.
   h) The person who gave the gift should do it legally through lawyers.

THE RECIPIENT:

The recipient's description must include the following:

1. The recipient's C-18 Vote Card or C-18 Vote/Tax Card Number and name.
2. The date of the gift received.
3. A description of the gift and serial/deeds numbers.
4. The value of the gift received.
5. The recipient should sign a letter accepting the gift through lawyers.

IMPORTANT NOTE:

When a Tax Clearance Certificate is issued by the Tax Department, it means that the gift is valid. The recipient will be responsible for any taxes.

PENDING LEGISLATION REGULATION 22: COMPANIES AND PRIVATE COMPANIES

COMPANY:

1. A person can be a partner in many companies.
2. Regulations 1 – 7 must be followed.
3. The company must manifest the total capital.
4. The partner will each write their name, Vote Roll Number, and their share in percentage.
5. The company will only write their Tax Category Number.
6. The tax will be paid by company.
7. The profit share will be transferred into each partner's account.
8. Each partner will fill in their own tax returns with their Vote Roll Number.

PRIVATE COMPANIES:

1. Family members can form a private company.
2. Regulations 1 -7 must be followed.
3. The company must manifest capital.
4. All partners will write their name, Vote Roll Number and their share percentage.
5. The company will only write their Tax Category Number.
6. The tax will be paid by the company.
7. The profit share will be transferred into each partner's account.
8. Each partner will fill in their own Tax Returns with their Vote Roll Number.

PENDING LEGISLATION REGULATION 23: TAX EVASION PENALTIES

Those who evade tax in any Tax Category will be penalised.

Those who evade tax by not supplying tickets/receipts in their Tax Categories will be fined (x times) according to their offences every month.

The fine/penalty will be based on the tax evaded:

(1)	First month	10X (times)
(2)	Second month	20X (times)
(3)	Third month	30X (times)
(4)	Fourth month	40X (times)
(5)	Fifth month	50X (times)
(6)	Sixth month	60X (times)
(7)	Seventh month	70X (times)
(8)	Eighth month	80X (times)
(9)	Ninth month	90X (times)
(10)	Tenth month	100X (times)
(11)	Eleventh month/time	Licence revoked for 5 years.

For example, in X Bus Services, a conductor tried to evade tax by not giving 20 passengers TicketTax Tickets worth $20 each, in the month of January. The conductor is caught in the act by the Tax Inspector. This is how the company will pay the penalty: 20 tickets @ $20 = $400, the tax @ 10% = $40 tax evaded. The penalty for the first offence is (January) 10x, therefore the fine will be $40 x 10 = $400. The second bus of the same company is caught in the same month (January) and pays a $600 fine. The penalty will be worked out monthly; as the X Bus Company had been caught twice in January, it will be counted as the first month, even if the company pays the fine 11 times in the same month. If they are fined in February, it will be counted as the second month.

Non-associated members: Those who are compulsorily required to join an association but are reluctant to join, will be subjected to a x50 penalty every time. Their licence will be revoked after the sixth month of penalties.

Associated members: Those who belong to an association will have their penalties mentioned in the next meeting (to shame them). After the eleventh transgression, they will be debarred from membership of the association, and their licence will be revoked for five years.

Note: The penalty will be for tax evaded and not the principal sum. For example, the bus conductor tried to evade the $2 tax, so it is this that counts, not the $20 charged to the passenger.

PENDING LEGISLATION REGULATION 24:COMPENSATIONS

It is the right of every citizen to seek compensation if they are genuinely wronged but in the present times it has become a trend amongst some unscrupulous people to sue and seek compensation for any loophole in the legislation.

The government has many departments and there are lots of civil servants working in it. The government as a body cannot keep track of each individual or individuals who supervise their department. In some cases, high handedness or excessive force is used on some person, resulting in the person suing the government or the government bodies for negligence, loss of business, loss of reputation, defamation and so forth. The government will not be accountable or responsible and will not compensate anybody for the unreasonable behaviour of their officials.

The government will not compensate simply because it has no money and also cannot be accountable for the government official's wrong doings.

The individual can drag the official[s] to court if they so wish. There will be Civil Servants Court.

The public/citizen cannot sue any government official[s] who are investigating a case even if s/he are found guilty or not.

The interrogation must be within the laws of the land and if there is excessive force then the investigating officials[s] will be liable if sued and not the government.

In some case where the government is directly involved and if there is a case to answer, the government will not compensate any person or party until the case has gone through the highest court of the land.

PENDING LEGISLATION REGULATION 25: RETAILERS

1. Exempt category. Non-licenced retailers (hawkers). Non-licenced retailers will have to use their Tax Card and C-18 Vote Roll Number for all purchases.
2. Licenced retailers. Licenced retailers will pay Provisional Tax as per their Tax Category in PIT-P.
3. Retailer importer. A tax rate of 6% will be payable to customs in Tax Category PIT-C1.
4. Retailers.

5. Bookkeeping will be compulsory for all licenced retailers.
6. Retailers cannot collect taxes.
7. Retailers will not be allowed to supply government departments.
8. Retailers will have to enclose their annual stock taking goods inventory pages with the Tax Assessments Form as per Regulation Number 42.
9. The retailer is to sell goods to the consumers for their own consumption.
10. If the retailer is caught selling goods to other retailers for resale, then their tax status will be changed from PIT-P TO PIT-C after paying penalties.
11. The Income Tax Department will have random stock checkups.
12. The Income Tax Department have the right to determine the tax status of the retailer if their volume of trade is high compared to their turnover.

PENDING LEGISLATION REGULATION 26: TRADEMARK BRANDS

APPOINTED AGENTS/FRANCHISE:

1. Worldwide trademark owners can appoint local franchise wholesalers or retailers to be their agents.
2. The company's appointment letter must be registered with the Trade Mark Registrar, clearly stating the brand name the franchise holder is to sell.
3. The validity of the appointment of the brand will be 24 months.
4. The appointment letter and the registration number should be advertised in two popular newspapers for six days.
5. A local company cannot register a foreign registered brand.
6. A local company may register their own brand and market it, provided that the spelling and sound are not similar to a popular trademark brand.
7. The appointed franchise agent wholesales will be placed in Tax Category PIT-C5.
8. The appointed franchise agent retailers will be placed in Tax Category PIT-P

PENDING LEGISLATION REGULATION 27: EXPORTS

1. All exporters require a licence, which can be obtained from the Ministry of Finance.
2. Only one bank is permitted for all exporter transactions.
3. A SPIT/EXP- Receipt will be issued (to the importer) once payment is received by the bank.
4. Foreign currency will be converted into local currency by the bank.
5. All export categories will send details of their exports to the Statistics Department.
6. All exporters must be members of an association or of the Chamber of Commerce.
7. The Statistics Department will release a report to the media regarding all exports, three months after the end of the financial year.

In developing countries, like any other country, exports are the main source of income.

Exports will be regulated by the Ministry of Trade and Industry/Agriculture, etc, along with the Ministry of Finance.

The exporter's Tax Category is SPIT/exports @ 5% by bank upon receiving payments from the importers.

For export categories, refer to page

The Export Licence is in Tax Category of SPIT/exports @ 5% by the bank.

PIT-C Tax Categories are required to issue a PIT-C-EX/Passport Number @ 5% for cross-border trade with the neighbouring country traders.

PENDING LEGISLATION REGULATION 28: CONTRACTORS

1. All contractors will be subject to their Capital Capacity Limit. The Capital Capacity Limit which is shown in the Tax Clearance Certificate which is the amount of work the contractor will be allowed to tender. So, supposing the contactor's TCC is $2,000,000, then the contractor cannot bid on any tender that is worth over $2,000,000.
2. The TCC will be valid for government contracts only.
3. All government contracts will be paid in stages, which will be identified in the plans.
4. Payment will be made after the completion of each stage of the plan or work.
5. Work will be inspected and approved by the City Inspector, the local MP where the contract is and the official of the ministry concerned before money is released to the contractor.
6. All building works must be guaranteed for 10 years by the contractor. All road works must be guaranteed for five years by the contractors.
7. If the government wishes to support indigenous companies, Regulation 28/1 can be waived.
8. The contractor's limit can be identified from their Tax Clearance Certificate.

PENDING LEGISLATION REGULATION 29: PARTNERS

1. All partners must register with the Registrar of Companies.
2. Each partner's share in the company must be clearly stated in terms of both amount and percentage.
3. The word 'company' must be used if there are two partners or more.
4. The share of each individual must be stated clearly on Form C-18.
5. Income Tax will be paid by the company.
6. Tax paid (from the company) should be entered onto each individual's capital account, based on their C-18 Vote/Tax Card Number.
7. A limited company's liability will be based on the partner's invested capital.
8. A Tax Clearance Certificate for the company will bear the amount of capital.
9. Private Limited Companies [family members] will follow the same rules of the companies.

PENDING LEGISLATION REGULATION 30: THREE TYPES OF NEW COURTS

1. Civil Servants Court
2. Corruption Court
3. Fast Track Court

CIVIL SERVANTS COURT

- The Civil Servant [government employee] will stand trial if he/she is a suspect.
- The Civil Servant will not be on duty until the trial finishes.
- The Civil Servant will have to fill in Form C-18 Pages 3 and 4 again for investigation purposes and then the salaries will have to be compiled to see if it tallies with the present possession of wealth. If it is in excess, it must be satisfactorily explained. If the excess is of 20 percent of their actual pay income totals then the person will not be guilty of any charge.

- If convicted the Civil Servantwill be dismissed immediately and no perks or gratuity and notice pay will be given and they cannot sue.
- The convicted person will not be employed by the government again and will not be able to represent any political party.
- The trial must finish within six months.

CORRUPTION CASES:

- All corruption cases must finish with judgement within six months.
- Buying time, wasting time or dilly-dally in court will not be allowed.
- The suspect must declare all their total capital by filling in Form C-18 rt 3 and 4. [Step 2] all the taxes paid must be totalled. [Step 3]the current capital value must be deducted with the previous value and if there is an excess it must explained satisfactorily.
- How the suspect got the contract must be established.
- How the fraud was done must be established.
- If convicted, the person[s] will be liable to pay back all the money with fines or;
- If the convicted person[s] fail to pay, then the court will forfeit or confiscate the assets or the person[s] may face jail sentences.

FAST TRACK COURTS:

- Fast Track Court cases must finish within three months or the reason be given by the court for failure to deliver a verdict. There should be re-trial.
- In the chambers there will be judge, the prosecutor and the defence lawyer who will argue the case by written statements. If they have a hitch or there is a technical point which needs to be established, then the court can set another day for trial. All three must agree to the judgement.
- Buying time, wasting time or dilly-dallying by either the prosecutor or the defence will not be allowed [in other words it will mean that the party dilly-dallying has no points to further the case]. Therefore, the ruling can be in favour of the opposition.

PENDING LEGISLATION REGULATION 31: IMPORTS BY CHARITIES AND RELIGIOUS ORGANISATIONS

1. There will be a 20% Customs Duty on all imports.
2. All religious and charitable organisations must have a licence.
3. All religious and charitable organisations will keep accounts and submit tax returns annually.
4. All religious or charitable organisations must register with the registrar, and supply a registered name.
5. The tax rate is 4%.
6. Charity and religious organisations are not tax exempt.

Note – As this system is wholly of accountability and transparency, therefore there will be no exemption of taxes; this is also to prevent corrupt practices.

PENDING LEGISLATION REGULATION 32: GOVERNMENT EXPENSES CONTROL

All developing countries should aim to control their expenditure and stop extravagances.

1. Government ministries will not procure goods or services valued at less than $100 on credit.
2. All government departments are to spend according to a monthly budget allocation.
3. All bills must be paid within 30 days of the date of invoice.
4. Any over-expenditure requirements must be authorised by a minister.
5. Governmental import of commodities must be cross-checked with similar local items; the imported item must be cheaper by at least 20%.
6. For transparency and statistics, the government department importing must pay a 20% custom duty.
7. No trader or company may import on behalf of the government.

PENDING LEGISTATION REGULATION 33: FOREIGN AID AND LOANS

Many developing countries depend on foreign aid for various reasons.

There are some countries whose cases are genuine, but many countries have developed the habit of relying on others, when actually they should be trying to manage their own budgets and be a self-reliant country.

One of the prerequisites of donors and the International Monetary Fund to borrowing countries should be the following:

1. All foreign aid or loans must be given a name and project number.
2. All projects must be advertised in two popular newspapers.
3. Bank accounts must be opened in the project's name with three signatories. The first signatory will be the donor's representative. The second signatory will be the minister concerned with the project. The third signatory will be the MP of the constituency where the project is based.
4. The contractor will be paid in stages, after the job is inspected and approved by the signatories.
5. When the project is finished, it must be advertised again in two popular newspapers.
6. Donors should not give cash but should finance developing projects in this way.

PENDING LEGISLATION REGULATION 34: PRICE-CONTROLLED ITEMS

HEALTH, EDUCATION AND AGRICULTURE ITEMS AND PRODUCTS:

In developing countries health, education and agriculture products must be pricecontrolled.

In many developing countries, hospitals are in a pathetic condition. There is limited medicine, as many of the stocks are sold to hawkers by doctors and pharmacy workers. A pharmacy must be established in all district hospitals run by private companies. The doctors will issue prescriptions to the patient which will have their C-18 Vote Roll Number. The patient will go the private pharmacy and will get free medicine if they are exempt and have no Tax Card Number. The Ministry of Health will pay the private pharmacy and keep a record of the payment made for each constituency C-18 Vote Roll Number. Retail pharmacies are allowed 20% profit on costs.

Note – This system will be better than not having medicines at all in the district hospitals, where corruption and robbery are rife.

In many developing countries basic education is not free; therefore, there is a need for affordable education materials.

Agricultural commodities must be price-controlled or subsidised, so that everyone benefits.

1. Local manufactured products are allowed 20% profit.
2. Wholesalers/distributors are allowed 10% profit.

PENDING LEGISLATION REGULATION 35: DEPRECIATION/APPRECIATION:

Valuations of motor vehicles and buildings will be based on real, sellable values.

1. Motor vehicles, cycles and boats need to be valued every year by official values, franchise firms, or by road traffic commissioners during MOTs or will be allowed 10% depreciation per annum.
2. All brick and mortar (buildings) will be valued every five years and will appreciate by 10%.
3. Industrial machinery will be re-valued or 10% will be allowed in depreciation per annum.
4. Fitting and Fixtures will be allowed 10% depreciations.

PENDING LEGISLATION REGULATION 36: STOCKS INVENTORIES

1. It is compulsory to enclose the full stock inventory pages with the IncomeTax Return Forms for Tax Assessments.
2. The IncomeTax Assessment will not be processed without the stock inventory.
3. The stock inventories will be kept in record for future investigation on 1] Bankruptcy; 2] Loses through acts of God, fire, storm, robbery or any other reason. The Form 13 is the police report that will be used to determine the loss in the event of any calamity.
4. The stock inventories will also be used to check when there is imbalance in accounting of purchases, sales and banking or when the figures are not tallying.

PENDING LEGISLATION REGULATION 37: IMPORTS

1. An Import Licence will be required.
2. The importer will use only one bank.
3. Annual FOREX quotas will be allocated with the licence.
4. Importers will use their Permanent Licence Number.
5. The importer is allowed to import from their designated group only.
6. The retailer importer Tax Category is PIT-P1 @.
7. New importers should apply for a licence if they have paid $10,000 tax or more over the year.
8. The FOREX quotas for new importers will start at $50,000 per annum.
9. There will be one Customs Duty Tariff.
10. Industries will pay 20% less on Customs Duty Tariffs.
11. No surveillance contracts will be awarded to companies by the government to monitor imports from exporting country.
12. Goods will be inspected and tallied at the Customs Border Depot. An inspection pass note will be given to importers, for them to remit FOREX.

13. Airline passengers bringing in goods exceeding their allowance will be subject to customs duties.
14. On airlines, non-accompanied baggage and parcels will not be awarded a personal allowance.
15. Road or sea/lake passengers bringing in goods over $2,000 of the normal allowance will have to release their goods through normal customs procedures.

The person will have to show proof of FOREX for unregulated imports.

Note – FOREX is foreign currency; mostly they are USA dollars.

PENDING LEGISLATION REGULATION 38: CAPITAL GAINS TAX

After filling in Form C-18 all the assets declared will have to be valued to their current market value. The newly valued capital will be deducted from the previous year's capital and the excess will be for Capital Gains Tax.

The Capital Gains Tax will take effect in the two years of amnesty period.

After the IncomeTax Department has assessed the Annual Tax Returns and has received payment it will issue a Tax Clearance Certificate, which will highlight the person's capital value.

PENDING LEGISLATION 39: FIVE-YEARLY RENEWAL OF FORM C-18

1. Form C-18 is mandatory on every citizen from the age of 18 years.
2. Every citizen will register at their constituency and get a Permanent Vote Roll Number.
3. The citizen will vote in their constituency.
4. Form C-18 must be renewed and filled every five years, and after a general election.
5. If a citizen wishes to change constituency, they may do so after five years or after the elections, following the appropriate procedures.
6. The renewed C-18 will be compared with the previous one [after five years] and the following determined:
   - Growth or decline of wealth.
   - That the growth of wealth tallies with the amount of IncomeTax paid.
   - An enquiry will be instigated if the capital is in excess of the tax paid.
   - An enquiry will be instigated if the capital cannot be tallied.
   A Tax Clearance Certificate will be issued after the new C-18 has been assessed by the Income Tax Department.
7. Form C-18 will be used for a population census every five years.

PENDING LEGISLATION REGULATION 40: CIVIL SERVANTS*/GOVERNMENT EMPLOYEES

(*Civil servant = a person working for and paid by the government in any ministry.)

1. Any civil servant or politician caught or suspected of corruption will be tried by the Special Court within 14 days.
2. They will be suspended from their post until they are cleared of charges.
3. If the civil servant is convicted, they will be sacked immediately and will forfeit their service contract payments and rights.

4. A convicted civil servant will face charges.
5. Civil servants who resist temptation will be rewarded with career progression.
6. Convicted civil servants will be barred from entering the Civil Service again.
7. Convicted politicians will not be able to compete in elections.
8. The police force or any team that recovers goods from any robbery will be rewarded with 10% of the value of recovered goods.
9. The government will reward customs officials for good work and receive 10% of the value of any recovered/confiscated goods.
10. The government will pay 10% of the fine collected to the traffic police as their reward.

If any civil servant is caught in corruption, then will remain in remand (jail) for fourteen days pending investigations.

PENDING REGULATIONS REGULATION 41: FREE MEDICAL SYSTEM FOR THE NATION

In developing countries the medical system is in a pathetic way where corruption is rife. The procuring officials with the unscrupulous traders will charge the government excessive prices on importation of medicine supplies. Thirty percent of the total value will be lost to them. When the medicines do come to the district hospitals, the corrupt duty officials will rob and sell it to hawkers from the 30 percent of the stocks. The hospitals will only receive 40 percent of the 100 percent, as 60 percent is lost to corrupt officials. Therefore, there are no medicines left in the hospital most of the time.

To stop the above malpractice, these new measures must be placed for exempt, civil servant and medical aid patients in the government hospitals:

1. The Ministry of Health will not order medicines but will pay the doctors/nurses/hospital care and maintenance.
2. The Government will allow commercial chemists or pharmacies to be set at the hospital or clinic.
3. The doctors will prescribe medicines to out/in patients, writing their Vote Roll Number only.
4. The pharmacy will write the Vote Roll Number of the patient and provide medicine and charge the Ministry of Health for it.
5. The pharmacy company will be allowed 20 percent profit.
6. The Constituency Office will record each patient by their Vote Roll Number.
7. All employees will require to be registered for medical aid by their employer with government hospitals or clinics.
   Admittance and treatment will be free but the medical aid will pay for laboratory and medicines
8. All fraud will be dealt with.
9. All civil servants and employees up to PAYE category [M] are entitled to free medical service at government hospitals.

Note. This will wipe out corruption and robbery and save the government more than 50 percent of the total medical expenditure and also create efficiency and regulatory in the hospitals and clinics.

PENDING LEGISLATION REGULATION 42: TAX EXEMPT – FREE MEDICAL, EDUCATION AND AGRICULCURE OUTPUTS

Tax-exempt categories 1-5 are entitled to free medicine, education, subsidised fertilisers and seeds.

The Ministry of Home Affairs that looks after all the constituency will have all the details of every tax-exempt citizen. They will publish a referral book with the names of all family members under the named constituency. The books will be distributed to all the licenced bookshops, district hospitals, private chemists and to all constituencies for subsidised fertilisers and seeds.

1. The citizen who visits the district hospital will show the C-18 Vote Card.
2. When the doctor prescribes medicines, they will refer to the 'Tax Exempt Book 20##' and write the name of the patient. If the patient is underage, the head of the house or guardian's C-18 Number will be written.
3. If it is an out-patient, they will take the prescription to the district chemist who will supply medicines for three days.
4. If it is an in-patient (admitted) the hospital in charge of the ward will bring in medicines on their behalf. If they are discharged, they will be given seven days medication to take with them.
5. The private chemist at the district hospital will issue an invoice for each patient. The hospital in charge will collect the medicines for the in-patients will sign the invoice. They will indicate the C-18 Vote Card Number, date, the name of patient, quantity of each medicine, the price of it and the total sum for that medicine. This may continue in the same way if there are other medicines. Finally, the total of all the medicines supplied is calculated.
6. The supplier (chemist) will make a list of all the invoices, total it and send it to the Ministry of Health to receive payment.
7. The Ministry of Health will record all the details of every invoice separately in each constituent's file, monthly. The file data will be sent to the concerned constituency.
8. Education materials for the children of Tax Exempts will be supplied by the appointed licenced bookshops. The supplier will note the C-18 Vote Card Number of the parent/guardian and also cross-check in the 'Tax Exempt Book 20##' if it is valid. The licenced bookshops will follow procedures as in 42(5), 42(6), 42 (7).
9. The Constituency Office will refer to the 'Tax Exempt Book 20##' to see how many bags of fertilisers and seeds the tax-exempt C-18 Vote Card Number holder is entitled. The constituent will buy at the subsidised price.

IMPORTS

IMPORTS

Anti-Corruption Measures for Imports

Imports are the second highest corruption area.

Corruption is so rife in this area that governments lose lots of revenue on Customs Duties every year.

The following measures will have to be taken to remedy the situation:

(A) Realistic Customs Duties.

(B) Higher pay for Custom Officers.

(C) Quotas of US$ to importers.

(D) Importers are only allowed to import from their designated group.

(1) The Imports Section (at the central bank) will have statistics of the previous years to determine the requirement of the particular item and its quantity. All excess should be denied permit.

(2) One bank must be used by importers to remit Forex* [USA Dollars].

(3) Random check of goods arriving in containers will be carried out.

(4) Customs Officers need to be sufficiently paid if the government expects honesty and dedication from the Customs Team. Their salaries must be generous; this will be key factor in obtaining good results.

The Customs Staff will think twice about losing a good job if they are paid well and know that they will be fired if any corruption is uncovered. Perks, overtime and bonuses must also be offered.

(5) If an importer is brought to book for an offence, the Investigating Officer(s) who have successfully helped in the prosecution (and upon conviction) will receive 10% of the value recovered.

If there is more than one officer, the 10% will be divided amongst them.

(6) To check on corruption, the government should rotate the postings of Customs Officers every year, from one border post to another.

(7) All Customs Officials will be placed on rotation when it comes to attending to the clearance of goods by importers. In this way, the unscrupulous importer will not know which Customs Official will attend to them.

Custom Officers who have shown and proved their dedication to duty will be promoted.

IMPORTS

Allotment of US Dollars to Importers

In developing countries US dollars are widely used for imports transactions.

(1) Imports Licences will also contain quotas of Forex* for the year. The trader will specify their designated Imports Group.

So, for example, if the trader is in Designated Group 2 for motor vehicles, then the trader will **not** be able to import from any other group. See Page 198 for groups listing.

(2) The Imports Licences will be presented in sequential serial numbers, in each designated group, and will be their Permanent Imports Licence Number.

(3) Forex will be provided to importers in their designated group. The trader is not allowed to import from outside their group.

(4) Allotment will depend on the previous year's imports and Customs Duty paid.

(5) If there is enough Forex in the country, 10% more will be added to the allotment for the next year.

(6) The importer will only be able to use one bank for import transactions and remittances.

(7) For the new importer, allocation of Forex will be based on the tax paid in the previous 12 months, or in the Tax Year Period, not to be less than $10,000. This will need to be proved by Tax Receipts. The allotment of US dollars to the new importer will start from $50,000.

(8) US dollars will be allotted to the importer upon availability.

(9) If there is a shortage of US dollars, all Importer Licence Holders will be trimmed of their quotas by 20, 30, 40, 50 or 60%. The new importers on the list will be put on hold until the situation improves.

(10) The Imports Provisional Income Tax will depend on the Importers Tax Category Rate.

* Forex = foreign currency.

IMPORTS

Designated group's Permanent Imports Licence Number:

(1) The requirement to import is to have a licence and permanent number of the designated imports group. (See page 198 for listing.)

(2) Application forms for an Imports Licence in the designated group will be available from the Reserve Bank.

(3) All questions in the application will have to be answered.

(4) The bank will fill in the figures of the amount remitted in the previous 12 months.

Only one bank will be allotted with Forex (US dollars) per licence.

(5) The applicant will have to disclose the items they wish to import and it must relate to the same designated group. So, for example, if the applicant wants to import vehicle tyres, vehicle batteries and vehicle spares which are in Group 2 and also wants to import computers and their accessories which are in Group 4, the computers (and accessories) will **not** be allowed as they are **not** in the **same** group of the licence.

(6) The licence application will go to the Reserve Bank's Forex Allocation Department for approval.

(7) The Reserve Bank will also send the application to the Imports Control Department to record the items the applicant wants to import in their designated group.

(8) The approved licence will contain a Permanent Number in its group.

(9) The new applicant's approval will only be considered if $10,000 tax has been paid in the previous 12 months. The initial allotment for the new applicant will start from $50,000 per year.

(10) For the renewal of licence, a new application form must be filled in using the Permanent Number of the group.

(11) The approved licence will contain the following information:

(a) The applicant's details.

(b) The Permanent Licence Number in the group.

(c) The beginning and expiry date of the licence.

(d) The Forex allotment for the year.

(e) Items to be imported relating to the group.

Note: Forex will be allotted upon availability.

IMPORTS

Annual quotas per licence in the designated group, and control on foreign exchange (US$)

The quotas for imports must not be regarded as anti-liberalised measures.

Quotas and import control are necessary for the gathering of precise statistics of imports in every item, and the value of foreign exchange required for it.

This is also to control the overflow of one item, where other required items are left out or cannot be imported due to lack of Forex.

Forex should be used by importers on their designated group only.

The allocation of Forex is not guaranteed and will depend on availability; it can be reduced.

An increment of 10% on the total value of the previous year's allotment of Forex will be allowed if there is any surplus.

A new Imports Licence Application will not be accepted if the Forex is low or if the applicant has not paid $10,000 Income Tax in the previous tax year.

The new importer will be given a $50,000 allocation for the year.

Items manufactured or processed locally must not be allowed to be imported. The local industry should be protected or, if there is a need for higher quality, then the Custom Duty should be increased so that the local product sales should be maintained.

IMPORTS

Foreign exchange currency (US $) Forex is to be allotted to one bank only.

Only one bank (of the importer's choice) will be allowed to deal with the transactions of foreign currency transfers and remittances.

The annual allotment of Forex by the Reserve or Central Bank will be allotted to one bank only.

GOVERNMENT PROCUREMENTS

The supplier to government procurements must have a licence and supply from their designated group.

IMPORTS

Realistic Customs Duties and Tariffs For All Imports:

Every year, the Minister of Finance in the annual budget sessions raises the tariffs of some items/commodities that are already high, in order to meet or hope to meet the budget targets.

The result is counter-productive, as traders or those affected try to avoid paying Custom Duties or work out a way around it. This also encourages unscrupulous traders to bribe and corrupt Customs Officials.

In this way the government loses out and does not receive any money at all.

If Customs Tariffs were realistic, the trader or the importer would pay the duties rather than take the risk, and the trader, as well as the government and the consumer, could benefit.

There will be one category of Customs Duty and tariffs for all.

Industries will pay 20% less Customs Duty.

There will be a special reduction of Custom Duties, at the rate of 20%, for: (1) medical supplies; (2) educational supplies; (3) charities and religious organisations; (4) agricultural supplies; (5) government imports.

IMPORTS

Designated Imports Groups

The importer will be allowed to import from their designated group only.
Group:

(1) Agriculture. All agriculture produce, fertilisers, farming machinery, etc.
(2) Motor vehicles. New cars, motor cycles, spares, etc.
(3) Bicycles. Bicycles, all cycles, spares, etc.
(4) Electronics. Fridges, computers, accessories, fans, heaters, etc.
(5) Hardware. All items.
(6) Furniture. All items (upholstery).

(7) Food. All items, cans, bottles, packets, biscuits, tinned foods, etc.

(8) Clothing. All items, clothes, shoes, etc.

(9) Beauty items. All items, cosmetics, soaps, toothpastes, etc.

(10) Health. Medicines, chemists, all health-related products.

(11) Stationery. Bookshops, printers, etc.

(12) Pleasure. All types of beers, whiskey, cigarettes, etc.

(13) Sports. All items.

(14) Industrial. Raw materials relating to the industry, machinery, etc.

(15) Dairy products. Milk, butter, etc.

(16) Livestock products. Meat, leathers.

(17) Petroleum products.

(18) Entertainment. Projectors, films, etc.

(19) Hawkers' items. household items, clothes hangers, pegs, bags, suitcases etc.

Note: There are lots of items (groups) not listed here.

IMPORTS

Inspection of imports to be cleared at the point of entry:

The inspection of goods must be carried out at the point of entry.

The importer must be present when the seal is broken from the container.

The inspection must tally with their documents.

Freight companies must have their depots at the borders.

If the inspection is clear, then an Inspection Pass Note will be issued to the importer for them to remit the Forex.

Precaution: Often Customs Officials are bribed at importer's warehouses, when they come to inspect the goods. To avoid this, the release of goods must be carried out at the Border Customs Depots or Special Custom Depots in the city.

The company freight depot may also be used as an inspection and clearance point.

IMPORTS

No surveillance company is to be contracted by the government to check prices and contents at the country of export.

No surveillance company should be contracted to check contents and prices at the country of export.

Surveillance costs are high, which results in passing the cost to the consumer.

Surveillance is not very effective and adds undue workload to the government's customs departments.

IMPORTS

Unregulated imports by passengers at borders/seaports/airports:

(1) Passengers are entitled to bring in goods from abroad up to a specified amount.

(2) All goods that passengers bring must be contained in their suitcases and hand luggage or cabin bag.

(3) A Customs Duty will be charged on the value of goods, minus what the passenger is entitled to.

(4) If the value of the goods is $2,000 over the entitled amount, then the goods will have to be released by the normal customs procedure.

(5) Unregulated importers will have to prove how the Forex was obtained.

IMPORTS

Bonded warehouses for industries will not to be allowed.

At the present time, governments allow industry as well as other traders to import and store their goods in bonded warehouses, to be cleared by paying Customs Duties and releasing it later on.

This practice involves lots of administrative work as well as surveillance.

In this system, bonded warehouses for either industry or the traders will not be allowed.

The government will allow the industry to pay 50% Customs Duties and release their raw materials/goods.

The other 50% will be paid in instalments over twelve months.

IMPORTS

Penalties for not paying Custom Duties:

First offence – penalty:

(1) Two times the Customs Duties evaded by the offender.
(2) The offender will have their Import Quotas reduced by 10% in Forex.

Second offence (after six months):

(1) Three times the Customs Duties value evaded by the offender.
(2) The offender will have their Import Quotas reduced by 20% in Forex.

Third offence (after 12 months):

(1) Four times the Customs Duties evaded by the offender.
(2) The offender will have their Import Quotas reduced by 30% in Forex.

Fourth offence (after 18 months):

(1) Five times the Customs Duties evaded by the offender.
(2) The offender will have their Import Quotas reduced by 50% in Forex.

Fifth offence (after 24 months):

(1) Ten times the Customs Duties evaded by the offender.
(2) No quotas will be given for two years.
(3) The quotas of the offender will be considered in the third year.

The offending corrupt official will be charged and sacked immediately.

As the penalties are very severe, the offender must be given the benefit of the doubt.

If there is only one offence in two years, it will be deleted from the records.

Customs Official(s) will share a 10% commission on penalties for successfully bringing a culprit to book.

CAPITAL GAINS TAX ON RE-VALUED ASSETS

CAPITAL GAINS TAX

Capital Gains Tax Assessment: Form C-18, Page 4
From the Assets and Liabilities Valuation Forms:

- Tax Assessments will fall at the end of the financial year.
- During the amnesty period, Valuation Forms will be used to determine the actual value of the asset.
- Valuation Forms will be signed and rubberstamped by the authorised person in the departments.
- The Valuation Form will have a net amount figure and no depreciation is allowed on it.

These categories will have a separate valuation form:

Business
Factories/warehouses
Shops
Properties/buildings
Residence
Flats/rooms
Hotels/rest houses/lodges
Holiday cottages/villas
Plots/lands/commercial or residential
Agricultural land
Vehicles, commercial
Vehicles, private
Boats/motorbikes
Industrial machinery
Investments
Cash on hand
Shares/bonds
Life insurance
Mortgages

These categories will have multiple entries in each valuation form:

> Trade goods inventories
> Fitting and fixtures
> *Debtors list
> *Banks' current and savings accounts
> *Pre-payments (local and foreign)
> Livestock inventory
> Precious stones/jewellery/paintings, etc
> Trusteeship/probate pending

Liabilities:

(1) Bad debts (with proof of court documents)
(2) *Overdrafts
(3) *Creditors (local)
(4) *Creditors (foreign)

*Full statement of accounts, to be accompanied with the form(s).

CAPITAL GAINS TAX

All the assets from 1 to 28 must be added to bring the grand total.
All the liabilities from 1 to 5 must be added to bring the grand total.
The grand total of 1 to 28 (assets) must be subtracted from the grand total of 1 to 5 (liabilities) to bring in the Net Capital for tax assessments.
Capital Gains Tax will apply to the amnesty tax assessment.

Amnesty Group A:

Already declared, but capital has been inflated by newly valued assets. Capital Gains Tax will be 20% on the difference between this new capital and the previous year's capital.

Amnesty Group B:

For those citizens who declare their assets in the amnesty period:
They will be taxed normally and **no** questions will be asked for three years*.
After three years, the tax payer must get a Tax Clearance Certificate for their assets, if they are clean.
If the assets were to be classified as ill-gotten gains from (1) corruption; (2) drugs money; or (3) robbery, the assets will be forfeited and the person will answer charges in a court of law.

Amnesty Group C:

For those who will fail to declare their assets in the amnesty period:
If their secret is out, they will be apprehended and they will be penalised by 33% of their assets' value. The penalty will be for **not** obeying the regulations. Income Tax will be assessed separately.

If the assets are from ill-gotten gains, they will be forfeited and the person will face charges. No assets over $500 can be sold in the amnesty period without a Tax Clearance Certificate.

Instalments:

If the Capital Gain Tax is less than $10,000, six months of instalments will be accepted.
If the Capital Gain Tax is less than $20,000, twelve months of instalments will be accepted.
If the Capital Gain Tax is less than $30,000, eighteen months of instalments will be accepted.
For up to $30,000, twenty-four months of instalments will be accepted.
For $100,000 and over, sixty months of instalments will be accepted.

CAPITAL GAINS TAX

What is the Assets and Liabilities Valuation Form?

The Assets and Liabilities Valuation Form is a form where each asset in Sequence 1 to 15 and 19, 20, 22, 23, 27 is to be filled in individually.

For example, Sequence 2 in the assets section is 'factories/warehouses (description)' and in the next column is the question 'how many'? if the reply is two, then two forms titled 'Factories/Warehouse(s)' will have to be filled in.

From Sequences 16, 17, 18, 21, 24, 25, 26, the form will consist of 10 lines in a page/form which must be filled as required and a second or third or fourth page/form may be used as required.

For example, No. 18 is an Asset Form for debtors. There will be 10 entries for the debtors in the form, and if there is a need for more forms to be used to accommodate all the debtor's entries, then as many forms as required should be used.

What is the purpose of a Valuation Form?

The government wants to record the actual value of an asset or the present market value.

To record this, it will be necessary to fill in a form separately to determine the value of each asset, signed by the Valuation Officer.

For example, a factory or warehouse bought or built in 1955 shows a value in the account books of $30,000. But its actual value in 2009 is $250,000 (the present market value). Therefore, the true value is in excess of $220,000, and it will have to be recorded as $250,000.

$220,000 and excess will be taxed in the Tax Category of Capital Gains Tax.

Capital Gains Tax will be applicable to Amnesty Groups A and B.
(Please refer to 'Amnesty').

Illustrations of the Valuation Forms are in the Capital Gains Tax Section.
(Refer to Page 219).

CAPITAL GAINS TAX

The new valuation of old properties/assets will be introduced and this will be taxed as Capital Gains Tax.

The government will offer a period of amnesty for all citizens to declare their hidden or non-recorded properties/assets.

Please refer to Amnesty:

The government will offer flexible instalments of payment on this tax after the assessment.

Form C-18/Page 4. The assessment of Capital Gains Tax will be based on the assets and liabilities submissions.

All assets will be added from the Valuation Forms (the new current market value).

Secondly, all the liabilities will be added up.

The grand total of assets will be subtracted from the total of liabilities, which will show a new capital.

New capital will be subtracted from previous capital, showing new capital gain.

Capital Gains Tax will be taxed as per the amnesty regulation applicable.

Important note:

To avoid paying taxes, some citizens might have used a family member's name to purchase assets.

To benefit in the Amnesty Tax Period, the person should transfer back to the actual owner(s) to avoid being classified into Amnesty Group C.

Capital Gains Tax will be for the amnesty period only based on the Valuation Assets Form.

The next Capital Gains Tax will be after five years, when the next C-18 Form will have to be filled in.

CAPITAL GAINS TAX

Assessment on assets and liabilities

Capital Gains Tax

Excess on capital – valuation forms:

Mr X has the following assets and liabilities according to his previous Tax Returns and the present valued assets and liabilities (according to the present Valuation Forms).

As Mr X is a tax payer and he had all assets and liabilities records in his account books. He will pay 20% on the excess that is the Capital Gains Tax, which will be $19,634, and will receive a Tax Clearance Certificate for the new capital value of $486,620**

This is the capital and Mr X's worth as per the date appearing on the Tax Clearance Certificate as capital 486.6K.

CAPITAL GAINS TAX

Assessment on assets and liabilities

First time Tax Payers with a Tax Category/Licence:

Mr A has been registered in the Tax Category TicketTax 1 or TTX/1, and has a licence and belongs to an association.

Mr A owns four passenger minibuses, and these are his declarations submitted on the Valuation Forms.

**(Amnesty period) Mr A will be charged Income Tax normally on the $48,150 and will receive a Tax Clearance Certificate for $48,150, dated in Capital 48.1K.

Regulation:

(1) The date is important and compulsory.
(2) The amount of 'capital' shown on the Tax Clearance Certificate is the true worth of the citizen's wealth/capital.
(3) The citizen who would like to purchase an asset with cash will require approval from the Tax Department if it is over the Tax Clearance Certificate amount.
(4) The Tax Clearance Certificate will be issued after every financial year end, or when the tax has been assessed and the payments received by the Income Tax Authorities.
(5) A Tax Clearance Certificate means that the tax has been paid. The date must be within 17 months, or else it will not be valid.

CAPITAL GAINS TAX

Assessment on assets and liabilities

Declaring hidden assets in the second year by the tax payer:
On the second year of the amnesty period, Mr X has second thoughts about his declaration and now wants to include a residential house, which he is renting (valued at $101,000).
These are his assets and liabilities in the second year:

1 commercial vehicle (newly valued)	$12,800
1 private vehicle (newly valued)	$ 8,800
Trade goods inventory	$522,400
Fitting and fixtures (newly valued)	$13,600
Debtors	$182,400
Cash in hand	300
Balance in bank	700
(Newly declared)	
House (rented)	$101,000

Liabilities:	$842,000
Creditors	$142,000

$700,000
Tax Clearance Certificate Number $486,620
$213,380
Normal tax will apply on $213,380

A new Tax Clearance Certificate for $700,000 will be issued, dated and entered in the records for capital 700K on the Tax Clearance Certificate.

CAPITAL GAINS TAX

Assessment on assets and liabilities

Declaring after the amnesty period is over.

Supposing Mr X declares his property after the amnesty period ends.

This will be regarded as non-declared, and the usual penalty of 33% will be imposed (on the declared assets).

The penalty on a property valued at $101,000 will be $33,663.33.

A Tax Clearance Certificate will be issued on this property so that proper deeds and ownership can be established.

Income Tax will be paid on the property in the following year at the value of $101,000.

CAPITAL GAINS TAX

New valuations for old buildings

The real purpose of establishing this system is so that everything becomes accountable.

There are lots of properties in the country that are old, but the value in the account books is of the year they were bought or built.

This will reflect a wrong capital value for the taxpayer.

The new regulation in this system will require buildings of over five years to be valued properly to the present sellable value.

Every five years, when Form C-18 needs to be filled in, the taxpayer must include the value form of the property.

The property value will be compared with the previous Valuation Form and the difference will be taxed as Capital Gains Tax.

The appreciation or depreciation will then be worked out in the capital accounts.

All properties will gain 10% in appreciation value.

CAPITAL GAINS TAX

INCOME TAX

REGIONAL INCOME TAX HEADQUARTERS:

Sorting the C-18 Forms received from the constituency

The Regional Income Tax Headquarters will be divided into District Tax Offices within the complex.

All the C-18 Forms received from the constituency will be sent to their respective District Office, to be assessed and put into their Tax Category and have their file opened.

The exempt category constituents will also be identified and slotted into their 1 to 5 Category; their status will remain in the District Constituency (Number) records until they are employed or when they start earning. They will then be put into the appropriate Tax Category.

The District Office within the Regional IncomeTax Headquarters will place the constituent in their Tax Category according to their business, profession or occupancy. They will be given a Tax Number of their Tax Category which will be followed by their Constituency Vote Roll Number. This will be sent to their constituency where they will be contacted to collect.

Correspondence to the Tax Payer will come from the Regional Income Tax Headquarters to their constituency.

The Regional Income Tax Headquarters will refer the Tax Categories to their District Tax Office or Treasury Cashiers.

The amnesty period will be for two years, and Capital Gains Tax will be assessed on it.

The next C-18 Form will be filled after five years or after the general elections.

The procedure of Form C-18 and the Regional Income Tax Headquarters is detailed over the following pages.

REGIONAL INCOME-TAX HEADQUARTERS:

From the constituency to the Regional Income Tax Headquarters

STEP 1:

Every person from age 18 years will be linked to the IncomeTax Department.

Every person will be graded into 20 Tax Categories.

(1) All C-18 Forms that have been registered and given C-18 Numbers at the constituency will be received by the Regional Income Tax Headquarters.

(2) At the Regional Income Tax Headquarters there will be separate offices, one for each district.

(3) C-18 Forms will be recorded at the Regional Income Tax Headquarters and then sent to the District Office within the Regional Income Tax Headquarters complex.

(4) The C-18 Forms received for a particular constituency will go to their District Office.

(5) In the Constituency District Office all the forms received will be categorised into 20 Tax Categories.

(1) PIT-C.
(2) PIT-P.
(3) Special imports.
(4) SPIT/professionals.
(5) SPIT/businesses.
(6) DUAL TAX/nature commodities
(7) SPIT/service charges.
(8) SPIT/ government procurements
(9) SPIT/investments.
(10) SPIT/exports.
(11) SPIT/government parastatals.
(12) SPIT/franchises.
(13) SPIT/commissions.
(14) SPIT/service providers.
(15) DUAL TAX/gambling.
(16) Ticket Tax.
(17) PAYE contracts.
(18) Numbered Revenue Stamps.
(19) Rentals.
(20) Exempt.

Files will be opened for all eligible tax payers according to their categories.

REGIONAL INCOMETAX HEADQUARTERS

From the constituency to the Regional Income Tax Headquarters

Step 2, Valuation Forms:

(7) If the citizen has indicated on Page 4 of Form C-18 that they have assets and liabilities, they will be sent the Valuation Forms of the assets and liabilities indicated.

(8) Valuation Forms will be sent for each asset as required; so, for example, if a citizen has two properties, then they will be sent two Valuation Forms, one for each property and so on.

(9) These are the assets that will have to be re-valued by the appointed agents for IncomeTax purposes

Form C-18, Page 4, Assets and Liabilities:

NO. 2.   Factories/warehouses
NO. 3.   Shops
NO. 4.   Offices

NO. 5.   Properties/whole buildings
NO. 6.   Residences
NO. 7.   Flats/rooms
NO. 8.   Hotels/rest houses/lodges
NO. 9.   Holiday cottages/villas
NO. 10.   Plots/land (commercial and residential)
NO. 11.   Agriculture/farm land
NO. 12.   Vehicles (commercial)
NO. 13.   Vehicles (private)
NO. 14.   Boats/motorbikes
NO. 15.   Industrial machinery/tools
NO. 17.   Fittings and fixtures
NO. 26.   Precious stones/jewellery

All the valuation forms must be signed and date stamped by the appointed Valuation Company or agents.

The Valuation Forms must be returned within the time specified.

INCOME TAX

These Valuation Forms will have multiple entries, and each entry must be accompanied by full detailed statements – which is marked*.

(16) Trade goods inventory (twenty entries in a page).
(18) Debtors list (twenty entries in one page).*
(19) Investments (five entries in one page).
(20) Bank accounts/savings account (two entries on a page).*
(22) Shares/bonds (two entries on a page).*
(23) Life insurance (two entries on a page).*
(24) Pre-payments foreign or local (three entries on a page).*
(25) Livestock/farming inventory.
(26) Mortgage amount paid up to date*.

Liabilities:

(01) Bad debts (full detailed copies of Court Case Number required along with a copy of lawyer's demand letters).
(02) Overdrafts/bank loans*
(03) Creditors*
(04) Creditors (foreign)*

The citizen must send back all the Valuation Forms by the date specified.

The citizen must **not** hide any information as this will amount to Tax Avoidance Penalties.

*statements

INCOMETAX

Step 3:

10. What tax officials will do with the:

(1) Temporary exempt.
(2) Self-sufficient farmers.
(3) Non-tax categories.

All C-18 Forms will be recorded at the Tax Office at the Regional Income Tax Headquarters, and then will be sent on to the Election Commission for the issuing of a C-18 Vote Card and the status of exemption.

11. What happens if the citizen does not have any assets or liabilities?

In that case, the Tax Official will categorise the citizen into one of the five exempt Tax Categories and open a file at the District Constituency Tax Department within the Regional Income Tax Headquarters as an exempt.

The Tax Official will file the Form C-18 in the exempt file in Section 1, 2, 3, 4 or 5 (for future reference) and issue a temporary Tax Exempt Certificate for the issuing of the C-18 Vote Card with a Vote Roll Number.

The Tax Clearance Certificate for the issuing of a C-18 Vote Card.

The Tax Official will issue a Tax Clearance Certificate and send the Certificate Number to the Election Commission for the issuing of a C-18 Vote Card.

The Tax Clearance Certificate will contain all the details of the Tax Category, the Tax Number and the relevant Permanent Licence Number (which will be obtained from the ministry concerned by the Income Tax Department).

The Regional Income Tax Headquarters will also issue a letter of authority to the tax payer for them to register at the Treasury Cashier as allocated.

The C-18 Vote/Tax Card will be used for obtaining driving licences, passports, purchasing goods as per its tax rate, voting, obtaining travellers' cheques, etc, etc.

The Election Commission will send the C-18 Vote/Tax Card with the Tax Clearance Certificate directly to the citizen or via their constituency.

REGIONAL INCOMETAX HEADQUARTERS:

12. Citizens with assets and liabilities:

Citizens with assets and liabilities will be sent the Valuation Forms for assets as indicated.
The forms must be filled in and the assets valued according to the present-day market value.
The Valuation Form(s) must be sent back on the date specified.
The Tax Officer will compile all the Valuation Forms in the file and will fill in an Amnesty Assessment Form.
This is how the assessment will be undertaken:

(1) If the citizen's capital is under $9,999, tax will be 0%.

(2) If the capital is over $10,000, normal tax rates will apply.

(3) Amnesty regulations will apply if it falls in the amnesty period of two years. Refer to Amnesty Regulation 19.

(4) The Income Tax Department will allow monthly instalments on Capital Gains Tax Payments for up to 60 months.

After all tax matters have been settled, the citizen will be issued with a Tax Clearance Certificate and a C-18 Vote/Tax Card issued as per their Tax Category.

Important note about this system:

The only difference in the Income Tax Department will be the creation of District Offices within the headquarters.

All files, records and assessments will be completed and filed at the District Constituency Office.

The District Constituency Office will provide all the detailed reports to the Assistant Tax Commissioner every month.

REGIONAL INCOME TAX HEADQUARTERS.

The District Office within the Regional Income Tax Headquarters

Registering:

(1) All the C-18 Forms received from the constituency will be scrutinised by the officials and will be placed into an appropriate separate file to be graded into their Tax Category.

(2) The tax exempt, self-sufficient farmers, and those in the non-tax category will be recorded and their C-18 Forms sent to the Election Commission for the issuing of a C-18 Vote Card.

(3) The exempt will have their file opened/recorded if they purchase any goods from the Tax Category PIT-C or obtain services from SPIT-.

(4) Citizens with **no** assets and liabilities will have their file opened in their respective exempt categories. The C-18 Form will be placed in a file.

(5) Citizens with assets and liabilities will be sent Valuation Forms for them to be filled in and returned. Some Valuation Forms will be assessed by appointed agents to find the actual value of the asset at its current market value.

(6) All Valuation Forms will be compiled in their Personal Tax File and will be assessed accordingly. If the assessment is in the amnesty period, then it will be assessed as per Regulation 19.

(7) The Tax Clearance Certificate will be issued at the end of assessment and the Tax Clearance Certificate will be sent to the Election Commission for the issuing of a C-18 Vote/Tax Card.

(8) The Regional Income Tax Headquarters will refer and allocate the Treasury Cashier, for them to open the file using their Licence Number.

(9) The Regional Income Tax Headquarters will also acquire the National Licence Number from the ministry concerned.

Recording the PIT-C/SPIT-/TTX/PAYE/monthly collection from the Daily Sales Sheet(s).

(1) Every month the District Office in the Regional Income Tax Headquarterswill receive Daily Sales Sheets from Treasury Cashiers.

(2) The officials in the Constituency Tax Office will record from the Daily Sales Sheets the entries of each line into their respective files.

(3) Every month end, the District Tax Office must release figures of the amount collected in the previous month. For example, the figures of January should be ready by end of February.

REGIONAL INCOME TAX HEADQUARTERS:

Assistant Tax Commissioner's Office:

The Assistant Tax Commissioner will receive a report from the District Constituency Office as to the amount of tax collected from each constituency every month end.

The Assistant Commissioner's Office's duty will be to tally the amounts totalled at the bank with the District Constituency Office's figures.

If there is any irregularity reported by the District Constituency Office, this will be passed on to the commissioner.

The Assistant Tax Commissionerwill send reports to the commissioner.

Commissioner's Office:

The commissioner will receive reports from the Assistant Tax Commissioneron:

- The total amount received from tax collections in **all** the districts.
- Any irregularities by tax payers which requires investigation.
- Any other matter that requires the attention of the commissioner.

The Commissioner's Office will release the figures of each constituency's tax collected to the Ministry of Finance.

Investigating Team:

This department will undertake the investigations into any irregularity.
If they have a case, it will be passed on to the Tax Prosecution Team.

Tax Prosecution Team:

The Income Tax Department will operate special courts set in each constituency on a certain day of the week.

If the defendant appeals against the case, then the case will be tried in the lower courts up to high courts.

DETECTING CORRUPTION

DETECTING CORRUPTION:

Random checks on Ticket Tax

Random checks by plainclothes inspectors can be carried out on Ticket Tax Categories. In Africa there are many minibuses that take on passengers without issuing any tickets or paying taxes.

With this system it will be compulsory for the buses to have Ticket Tax Tickets. The inspector could go on for a ride and see if the conductor gives a Ticket Tax Ticket for the fare paid or not.

The second line of investigation will be to see if the bus is registered in the Ticket Tax Category, and the numbers of the tickets must match with the Treasury Cashier's Consent Receipt.

In the same way all other Ticket Tax Categories could be checked.

Tax Category PIT-C and SPIT (all categories):

The first thing to check with the PIT-C and SPIT (all categories) is the Daily Sales Sheet and the PIT-C/SPIT Receipts Entry. The numbers must be in sequence. Sales for the day, and of the previous day, must be checked also, to see if they are in proper order on the day'sDaily Sales Sheet.

The second step would be to wait for the customer who has bought goods from the PIT-C/SPIT to come out of the commercial premises, and the Tax Inspector will demand to see their Sales Voucher and PIT-C/SPIT Receipt. This is to check if the Sales Voucher and the PIT-C/SPIT receipt has been issued or not.

Late submitting of Daily Sales Sheets:

The Tax Inspector will be sent to the tax payer if their Daily Sales Sheetis not received by the end of the following month. For example, January'sDaily Sales Sheet, if not received by 10th February as standard deadline, will wait till end of February and take action in March.

The tax payer should be given a booklet on this subject and be warned that the second late submission will result in penalties.

Income Tax Investigating Team:

If a non-licenced person deposits large amounts of money in a bank account, more than the average amount usually deposited, this must be reported to the Income Tax Department's Investigating Team by the bank. The team will fully scrutinise and assess the situation privately, and if there is any suspicion or anything odd about it, the monies will be ordered to be frozen and the person will be asked to explain.

If the person(s) withdraws lots of money in cash from the bank, the bank must refer to the account holder or the department about the withdrawal to check if it is OK.

Lots of government/trader's money has been lost in this way.

DETECTING CORRUPTION:

Contractors:

This is an example of two systems, the present and the new.

For example, in the present system the Ministry of Education wants a school block to be built and the ministry advertises for tenders. There are many tenders submitted, but the tender that is passed and approved is **not** based on who is the cheapest or who is the best, but which contractor has offered more bribes.

Supposing the contract was for $10 million. Of this $10m, the contractor will have to bribe and also have to build the school block. If the school project ever gets completed, it will be of sub-standard quality with no guarantee because the contractor would have cut corners to make more profits.

Now let us analyse the difference it would make if the **new** system were in place.

For example, the contract for building the school block is for $10m. In this system there will be a plan and the work will have to be completed in stages. For this project there will be five stages.

The contractor will start work in stages and will be paid according to the stage completed and **not in advance**, as per Regulation No. 28.

After completing Phase 1, the contractor in Tax Category SPIT/BUS11 will receive $2m, of which the contractor will pay 4% SPIT- (for government contracts) which is $80,000. The work of Phase 1 will be thoroughly checked by the city inspectors, the donor country's representative, the resident MP and the officials of the ministry concerned, and in this way the project will be completed.

The contractors are allowed to make a 20% profit on any government project or services as per Regulation No. 8.

It would be difficult to offer bribes in this new system, as the profit margin is controlled.

Now let us analyse the options the officials will have to receive commission (bribes) from the contractor in the new system.

There is only one way that this can be done and this is that the city building inspectors, resident MP and an official from the Ministry of Education all conspire with the contractor to certify the inferior work or substandard work and divide the spoils, on a phase-by-phase basis.

Under Regulation 28/4, the newly constructed building will carry a 10-year guarantee. The contractor will be responsible for any inferior work, and the cost of rebuilding the damaged portion of the building.

The three-way partnership in bribery will never work (as it is bound to be discovered).

Any government official **or** politician caught in a corruption case and proved guilty must be sacked from their position as per Regulation Numbers 40/1 & 40/2 leading to 40/3.

DETECTING CORRUPTION:

High level corruption – this is one of the many corrupt practices:

A developing country had embarked on a scheme of free education. Vast quantities of exercise books and pencils were required. The Minister of Education saw this as an opportunity to import the items and enrich himself by conspiring with the exporter to inflate the prices of exercise books and pencils and deposit the excessive amount in his foreign bank account. This was discovered by the Anti-Corruption Bureau, as the cost of each exercise book and pencil worked out at $3 each. If the same product had bought locally, it would have cost 35c each.

Now let us analyse what difference it would have made if this system were in place.

The ministry would have asked licenced suppliers to supply the exercise books and pencils. If the price locally was higher or the quantity was **not** available, only then could the ministry have imported the items.

If the exercise books and pencils were supplied locally, it would have cost 20% more than importing.

If the exercise books and pencils were imported by the ministry, it would cost 28c or less.

The evidence in the court case would have been the invoice of the exporter, with the quantity - price and total amount. The area to check would be the quantity and the price locally and the total amount. The difference between the two is the amount that was pocketed corruptly.

The above incident was an easy catch, because the prices of the items are known. **But** how can corruption of a very high scale be detected and the culprit brought to justice with evidence?

For example, a licence has been granted for the establishment of a new mobile phone network. The amount of the bribe given was enormous. After three years, the officials were caught and investigations got underway. This is how the investigation should be conducted and evidence produced:

(1) The total capital of the minister during the amnesty period. (Form C-18)
(2) Year 1: Add the minister's profits as per the assessed IncomeTax Accounts to the amnesty period.
(3) Year 2: Add the minister's profits as per the assessed accounts to Year 1.
(4) Year 3: Add the minister's assessed profits to Year 2 to bring in the grand total of the minister's (worth) **capital** which will be shown on the Tax Clearance Certificate.
(5) The minister must again fill in Form C-18 Pages 3 and 4 to bring about the **present capital**. (The filling in of Form C-18 will be for investigating purposes only.)
(6) Deduct No. 5 from No. 4, and if there is an excess, it is from corruption.

Note: If it is a clear case of corruption, the official's assets should be confiscated. If the amount confiscated is **not** enough, then the money has been sent abroad; the ex-minister will then be ordered (by court order) to return it or face a jail sentence.

BENEFITS

BENEFITS:

Let's see how much this system will benefit the country and how much surplus will be added to the Annual Budget without raising any taxes.

So, for example, the Annual Budget is $100,000,000; this is what will be added, without raising taxes.

Benefit No. 1.

TAXING ALL THOSE WHO EARN

In developing countries there are thousands of unregulated, non-licenced retailers who do **no** bookkeeping and pay **no** taxes.

With this system they will **all** have to do their purchasing with their Tax/Vote Card Number and will have to pay Provisional IncomeTax as per their Tax Category.

The statistics show that only 14% pay taxes. With this new system there will be 90% tax payers.

Therefore, the annual budget surplus will double or more.

Benefit No. 2.

Stopping the black economy*

*Black economy = the part of a country's economic activity which is not recorded or taxed by the government.

In developing countries this is the **main** loophole in the avoidance of paying taxes.

The registered and licenced tax payer who undertakes bookkeeping is the main culprit, as they buy and sell their goods with **cash money** and do not give or take any Sales Vouchers. They pocket the profits without recording anything in their account books. Only transactions done through the bank are shown in the account books.

Within this new system, **all** transactions will be shown, because **all** transactions will have a Sales Voucher as well as a PIT-C Receipt Number. If **no** Sales Voucher or PIT-C Receipt is issued, the PIT-Collector will face stiff penalties.

This will put a stop to **all** malpractices, and this system will bring in more surplus revenue.

Therefore, the anticipated increase on budget surplus could double or more.

BENEFITS:

Benefit No. 3.

Procurement of goods and services by the government

This is the biggest corruption area in developing countries. Most of the high government officials take this as a chance to enrich themselves and their families by taking hefty bribes from unscrupulous traders or contractors, to give them contracts.

This highly corrupt area will be properly regulated. The suppliers will be allowed to make only a 20% profit, as per Regulation No. 8. Procurements by government ministries will be supplied by **all**licenced suppliers equally in their supply group. No payment will be made upfront.

Assumption: This is the highest corruption area. If this can be prevented by using Regulation 8, then the country will save and add to the budget enormously

BENEFIT No. 4.

Importers:

There are many importers who evade paying Customs Duty by bribing customs officials or releasing their goods on lower tariffs or smuggling through the borders.

In this system, the importer will **not** indulge in evading Customs Duties, as this will work out to their disadvantage in the long run. The less they pay towards Customs Duties, the less foreign exchange quotas they will receive.

Assumption: If this can be achieved then the country could add more to their budget surplus.

BENEFIT No. 5.

Monthly cash flow:

Many developing countries borrow money on interest from their own citizens and banks, paying them higher interest rates then the local banks. The monies are borrowed **every** month for a period of three to six months. The next borrowing by the government will pay for the maturing debts with interest, and the cycle continues.

The monthly interest payouts are enormous.

The main intention of this system is to create cash flow every month from various Provisional IncomeTax collections.

This will save the country from paying interest. The savings will be astonishing.

BENEFIT No: 6.

Revaluation of Assets in Amnesty Period: (Two years).

As the buildings and assets will be valued to the present market value, this will generate lots of revenue on the Capital Gains Tax.

The revenue increase in the two-year amnesty period will be enormous.

BENEFIT No: 7.

Low-Cost Housing:

Low-cost housing will be an infinite benefit to the poor villagers and town dwellers living in mud/thatched huts and shacks.

BENEFIT No: 8.

Compulsory Bonus to the Employees:

The compulsory bonus will benefit the employees greatly, in this system.
This will also eliminate workers' strikes and create loyalty and dedication.
The benefit will be no unnecessary payouts.

BENEFIT No: 9.

Transparency, Accountability and Proper IncomeTax Collections:

In **all** the pages of this manual, there is transparency, accountability and a mechanism of collecting taxes, the three qualities that are most lacking in many developing countries.

FORM C-18   PAGE 1

CONSTITUENCY / ELECTORAL COMMISSION / MINISTRY OF HOME AFFAIRS

C-18 NUMBER...............CONSTITUENCY.......................

DATE OF REGISTRATION.............................NEXT REGISTRATION...................

(1)...........................   ....

....

(First name)   (Second name)   (Father's name)   (Surname)

(2) YOUR DATE OF BIRTH ....

(For all persons living in this country)

(3) YOUR PLACE OF BIRTH ....

  (If born in this country)   (Constituency)   (District)

STATISTICS.   (PLEASE REFER TO CHARTS)

EDUCATION LEVEL:..........................CAN YOU READ/WRITE/SPEAK ENGLISH?

HEALTH.. HAVE YOU BEEN HOSPITALISED?...........

PRISON........................... ....HAVE YOU BEEN IMPRISONED?......................

BLOOD GROUP (OPTIONAL)..

HIV/AIDS : HAVE YOU TESTED YES/ NO.......RESULT:...NEGATIVE/ POSITIVE

IMMIGRANTS.

(*) YOUR RESIDENT STATUS..

(*) FILE NUMBER..

(*) YOUR NATIONALITY (PASSPORT YOU HOLD)......................................

(*) PASSPORT

NUMBER...EXPIRY............................

POPULATION CENSUS.

ARE YOU THE HEAD OF THE HOUSE ?   YES / NO

LIVING IN ONE HOUSE.

NAME OF PERSON   M / F   D.O.B.   AGE

1.

2.

3.

4.

5.

6.

7

(+) UNDER 5 YEARS	(+) UNDER 18 (NOT EARNING)	(+)UNDER 18 (EARNING [Trustees]	[X] PARENTS OR OVER 18 AND EARNING	[X] DISABLED OR OTHER RELATIVE /ORPHANS	TOTAL LIVING IN HOUSE

Note; Over 18 years will not be counted in census living in the same house

NOTE:-

(+) SHOULD BE COUNTED IN CENSUS.

(X) SHOULD NOT BE COUNTED.

Signature.	Thumb Mark	MP Signature	Vote Roll Number

FORM C-18.   PAGE 2

NATIONAL HOUSING AND WATER FUNDING.
RENT TAXATION AND RENTAL ASSOCIATION.

MARK 'X' IN THIS BOX IF YOU LIVE IN A MUD OR THATCHED HUT	MARK 'X' IN THIS BOX IF YOU ARE HOMELESS

LOCATION/VILLAGE...DISTRICT NH&WF..............................
QUEUE SEQUENCE NUMBER FOR LOW COST HOUSES...
....

HOUSE TYPE.   (PLEASE REFER TO CHART)

(WRITE HERE)	Mark 'X' here for free / non rent QUARTERS)

LIVING IN OWN RESIDENCE.

PLOT NUMBER..........................DEED NUMBER............STREET............................
LOCATION CONSTITUENCY..
CITY RATES REF NUMBER................................WATER METER NUMBER................
PREVAILING RENT PER MONTH $................/00. (SEE CHART 'HOUSE TYPE ')
....

TRADING / EARNING FROM OWN PREMISES.

PLOT NUMBER: .... DEED NUMBER:.................. STREET.......................
LOCATION/ CONSTITUENCY...
CITY RATES REF NUMBER.......................................WATER METER NUMBER.......................
SQUARE FEET / METERS AREA...
PREVAILING RENT PER MONTH $.....................(00. (SEE CHART; COMMERCIAL PROPERTY/
PREMISES)

....

RENTED RESIDENCE.   RENTED COMMERCIAL

RENTED RESIDENCE	RENTED COMMERCIAL
1. RESIDENCE TYPE...	1. COMMERCIAL TYPE...
2. PLOT NUMBER...	2. PLOT NUMBER...
3. STREET...	3. STREET..........
4. LOCATION/ CONST.........	4. LOCATION/CONST....
5. WATER METER NO......	5. SQUARE FEET/METERS
6. RENT PM...............	6. RENT PM...............
7. LANDLORDS C-18 NO:................	7. LANDLORDS C-18 NO:..............
8. LANDLORDS NAME/ADDRESS	8. LANDLORDS NAME/ADDRESS
....	....
....	....

FORM C-18   Page 3

DEPARTMENT OF INCOME-TAX. DATE........../......../.........

NAME...,TAX NUMBER ....
C-18 NUMBER.......................................CONSTITUENCY...............................
HOW MANY PARTNERS ?..................... COMPANY NAME...

NUMBER: TICK;	TAX CATEGORY:		TAX RATES
1	**PIT –C**	CUSTOMS / INDUSTRIES / WHOLESLAERS /	V
2	**PIT – P**	RETAILERS / NON LICENSED RETAILERS /	4%
3	**PIT – SI**	[CUSTOMS] MEDICAL / EDUCATION / AGRICULTURE /	20%
4	SPIT – PRO	PROFESSIONALS WITH PRACTICES	10%
5	SPIT – BUSINESS	BUSINESSES NOT IN CATEGORY PIT-C & PIT-P TRANSPORT / PVT SCHOOLS / HIRE /	10%
6	SPIT – SERVICE CHARGES	BANKS / RESTUARANTS	10%
7	SPIT – SERVICE PROVIDERS	BURIALS / SECURITY / GARAGES	10%
8	SPIT - SUPPLIERS TO GOVERNMENT PROCUREMENTS		04%
9	SPIT – INVESTMENTS	PROPERTIES/ LANDS / STOCKS /SAVINGS	20%
10	SPIT – NGO PARASTATALS	WATER / ELECTRICITY / TV / PHONES	10%
11	SPIT – COMMISSION	AIRLINES / AUTION / BROKERS	10%
12	SPIT – RENTALS	PROPERTIES AND OTHERS	15%}
		NATIONAL HOUSING & SOCIAL WELFARE	05%}
13	NATURE COMMODITIES [DUAL TAX] BUYER SPIT-#		10%
		SELLER [SELF SUFFICIENT FARMER] PIT-C	04%
14	GAMBLING	[DUAL TAX] PUNTER WINNER PIT-C8	10%
		CASINO WINS SPIT-	10%
15	NON LICENSE HOLDER	HAWKERS / RURAL RETAILERS / SELF SUFFICIENT FARMERS	04%
16	EXPORTS		
17	PAYE & PAYE CONTRACTS		AS PER TAX SCHEDULE
18	TICKET TAX TICKETS	ALL ENTRY BY TICKETS	10%
19	NUMBERED REVENUE STAMPS	SALE OF SECOND HAND ITEMS	10%
20	EXEMPTS	HOUSEWIFE / STUDENTS / UNEMPLOYED / DISABLED	N/A

| (1) Dependant staying with family and not earning. | (2) Dependant staying with family and studying. | (3) Staying with family long time sick/ disabled. | (4) Dependant old age retired with no assets. | (5) Self sufficient farmer. |

FORM C – 18 PAGE 4

DEPARTMENT OF INCOME TAX .

ASSETS.

NUMBER.	ASSETS DESCRIPTION.	NUMBER OWNED	SOLE OWNERSHIP	PARTNERSHIP
1.	BUSINESS..			
2.	FACTORIES/WAREHOUSES..			
3.	SHOPS...			
4.	OFFICES..			
5.	PROPERTIES/BUILDINGS...			
6.	RESIDENCES...			
7.	FLATS/ROOMS..			
8.	HOTELS/REST HOUSES/LODGES/......................................			
9.	HOLIDAY COTTAGES/VILLAS..			
10.	PLOTS/LAND(COMMERCIAL/ RESIDENTIAL)......................			
11.	AGRICULTURAL LAND..			
12.	VEHICLES: COMMERCIAL..			
13.	VEHICLES: PRIVATE...			
14.	BOATS/MOTORBIKES..			
15.	INDUSTRIAL MACHINERY (INVENTORY)			
16.	TRADE GOODS (INVENTORY)..			
17.	FITTINGS & FIXTURES...			
18.	DEBTORS			
19.	INVESTMENTS (INVENTORY)..			
20.	CASH IN HAND..			
21.	BANK ACCOUNTS/SAVING ACCOUNTS................................			
22.	SHARES/BONDS..			
23.	LIFE INSURANCE..			
24.	PRE-PAYMENTS (LOCAL/FOREIGN).....................................			
25.	LIVESTOCK/ FARMING (INVENTORY)..................................			
26.	PRECIOUS STONES/JEWELLERY (INVENTORY).....................			
27.	MORTGAGE AMOUNT PAID UP TO DATE INCLUDING INTREST.........................			
28.	TRUST (PROBATE DATE APPLIED)......................................			

LIABILITIES.
1. BAD DEBTS..
2. OVERDRAFTS (ALL ACCOUNTS)...
3. CREDITORS (FULL LIST)..
4. CREDITORS (FOREIGN) (FULL LIST)..................................
5. OTHER...

NOTE:- There will be one supplementary form for each asset 1 to 15 and 20/22/23/27. The rest are of multiple entries in each supplementary form.
NOTE: - These forms must be date stamped and signed by the valuation official(s).
Assets- 2/3/4/5/6/7/8/9/10/11/12/13/14/15/17. Accountant will sign 16/20/25/26
Bank will sign 24/27
This supplementary form must be accompanied by detailed statements
Assets- 18/ 19/21/22/23/.
Liabilities – 1/2/3/4.

* All Assets 1 to 27 must be filled and if 28 is applicable write the date here applied for probate.

Printed in the United States
by Baker & Taylor Publisher Services

Printed in the United States
by Baker & Taylor Publisher Services